ALL OR NOTHING

ALL OR NOTHING

Miriam Malach

atmosphere press

All or nothing at all
Half a love never appealed to me
If your heart never could yield to me
Then I'd rather have nothing at all

From the song "All or Nothing at All"
Music by Arthur Altman,
Lyrics by Jack Lawrence

PART I: PARIS

Alex and Marty checked into a student hotel on the *rue Jacob* after a long train ride from Milan and desperately wanted a drink. It was fall 1951, their first time in Paris. What they wished for, embossed in their imagination, was a café overflowing a sidewalk with small tables serviced by waiters in frock coats where they could relax, have an unfamiliar aperitive, maybe a Pernod, a sort of modern version of absinthe which somewhere Marty had read about, and simultaneously absorb the scents and sights of the as yet unfamiliar city. They stumbled into the first café they came upon as they turned the corner from the *rue Jacob* and approached the *Boulevard Saint Germain*. They contentedly sat down at the first table that beckoned. It was not entirely a coincidence, as it turned out, that a slim blond with dancing gait would amble by the popular *Café des Deux Magots*. What Marty forever remembered was the sound of the unexpectedly American voice tinged with excitement that broke into his consciousness from the boulevard side of the terrace when he least expected to encounter a face familiar to either him or Alex. Marty turned to Alex with a puzzled expression when he sensed she was coming towards them. Alex, embarrassed, shrugged his shoulders as if to disclaim responsibility before rising to acknowledge her.

"You're here?" The question was directed at Alex. "Hadn't the vaguest notion I would ever run into you in, of all places, a café in Paris." Without waiting, she turned to Marty and said, "I'm Sonia." She was a handsome woman happy to be with "her crowd."

Marty bowed his head in greeting. He was puzzled that Alex made no effort to introduce her but was surprised by the nature of the exchange. He and Alex had been lovers since their junior year in college. Sonia, he figured, had to be a mere acquaintance. And yet it had to be more, for she so confidently approached the tall blue-eyed blond with the tumbling lock of hair sitting next to him in a foreign city. She came with more than mere admiration for a handsome man; she radiated joy. "I'm Martin," he said, responding to her introduction, and smiled.

"I had no idea you would be here," said Alex. He pulled up a chair for her. "Come, tell us what you are doing in Paris."

She sat down between them as if she could not believe she was again with Alex. "I'm on a Fulbright. Sorry, didn't have a chance to alert you when I last saw you. I've been here since mid-September. And you?"

"Just touring. Arrived about an hour or so ago. The European tour before Marty and I settle down to making our way in the world." Alex looked expectantly at her. "You were at Columbia, so I assume you are finishing…"

"Yes," Sonia said. "I'm working on a dissertation on Marcel Proust's work as my thesis. I'm sure you've have heard of him."

Alex responded to her by laughing. "My books generally relate to accounting; literary books are his department," he said, indicating Marty with his head. But he continued, "As you know, I do dabble."

Marty suspected Alex knew more about Sonia than was possible from a casual meeting. He listened to their conversation while surveying the scene before him. He caught the eye of a waiter, who reminded him of the reason they were there. He said, "We better order before we lose the waiter. Sonia, what's your wish?"

"A Martini, that is a French Martini, please—not the gin and vermouth variety."

To Alex, Marty said, "O.K. with you if we order the same?" He was confident Alex would enjoy what he took to be an aperitif neither had drunk before. He had forgotten about Pernod.

Marty hailed the waiter and, ordering in halting French, was unable to decide if the "in" in Martini should or should not be nasal. It tumbled out, in his best Americanese, with a nasal, "in". It was wrong but too late to correct. He had not yet learned of its Italian origin. The waiter understood. Nobody was embarrassed. Sonia, who had to be more fluent in French than either he or Alex, made no effort to correct his mispronunciation. He decided he liked her. He said, "Proust, yes, I suppose so, but I will admit I haven't read him."

Marty was struck by the way her blue eyes sparkled as she nodded. "Yes, I think it is a good subject. I needed to justify my application and he met it handsomely. You see, I applied late and was afraid I'd never make it. But fortunately, I did. And to top it off I meet you."

Turning to Alex, she said, "That's the reason I never told you. When we met in New York I had no idea Paris was in my future."

Marty's thoughts wandered away from the conversation. He tried hard not to think of what Alex may have been keeping from him. Marty needed to trust. They knew they had to keep up appearances in a society that did not accept same sex lovers. He suspected Sonia had no more than book knowledge, if that, of such relationships and could hardly be expected to have encountered any in her social circle. Although he could not be sure, he felt confident of his judgment. He let the subject rest. In the meantime, he enjoyed the buzz floating overhead from the mass of humanity conversing in a variety of languages in the terrace tables around him, a slow river melding with the traffic sounds from the intersection facing the church of *Saint Germain*. He found the soft light of the terrace soothing as it flowed onto the streetlight beaming on the sidewalk around the corner.

The drinks suddenly appeared on the table, and Marty became conscious of Sonia welcoming him with a glass in her hand. She seemed to be inspecting him, making him self-conscious. She radiated kindness and he tried to respond in the same vein. He started to sip the wine slowly, savoring its bite. It was satisfying and endeared the woman he had just met to him. "Anything particular you intend to do?" she asked.

Marty couldn't help but chuckle because he had no ready answer. He was a couple of inches shorter than Alex, swarthy with jet-black hair and distinctive eyebrows, one would have thought incised. They sometimes gave the impression of being differently flavored, one chocolate and the other plain vanilla. Marty didn't always appreciate it, but that night it suited him. He felt separated from Alex.

Neither responded. Sonia continued, "The chances are we each bring a particular Paris with us. We have our own vision of what to expect. I have my Proustian world. What's yours?"

Marty scanned his memory for what he had absorbed from Henry James to Scott Fitzgerald, Hemingway and Gertrude Stein. He had, however, not given the subject much thought and was in a quandary on how to respond. He did not want to sound arrogant. He said, "I would be happy just being a loopy tourist, getting a feel of the life of the street, slogging through museums, visiting churches, and admiring monuments. I will stop in between for coffee and rest my feet while I watch the parade of people passing by. If we happen to wander up to Montmartre, I will try but not too hard to find Picasso's *Bateau Lavoir*. If we do track it down, I will happily visit, if allowed, and dream. Otherwise just being around there will be pleasure enough. I don't think we've given much thought to how long we will stay, so we will have to decide as we go along what we want to do. It should be fun to be unstructured, unpremeditated, unschooled in a way, don't you think? Alex, do we want to go out of town? I would love to take a few days on the Loire to see the famous chateaux. Does this sound like a good plan?"

"Very appealing. May I join you?" Sonia said. She looked expectantly at Alex.

"Sure, anytime. Incidentally," Alex said. He sheepishly looked at Marty as if uncertain whether to proceed. "You being almost a Parisian, do you happen to know of a better hotel than our little hovel around the corner? Reasonable, of course."

"Strange you should ask," Sonia said. She looked inquisitively at Alex and Marty as if to ask for a description of the type of accommodation that would please them. She did not appear to have received a reply when she proceeded to tell her story.

"I have an idea. First, however, let me digress for a moment. I will be here until next summer, when I go back to submit my dissertation, which I hopefully will have completed. I lucked out and rent an apartment from a French family I happened to meet because of a telephone call I made on behalf of a friend to her relatives here, a huge extended family figuring out how to dispose of an inheritance, the said apartment. A fortunate accident is what it is."

Marty wondered what the point could be. He became uncomfortable and wondered if she was aiming to split them up.

Sonia continued with a smile and said, "They are so indecisive about what they eventually want to do with it that I am confident I can stay out my time. The furniture is haphazard but adequate. It has four rooms lined up like tipsy ducks, a bathroom attached to a long corridor and a kitchen tacked on. Although there are quirks, it is quite comfortable. It is an unusual find in a city where housing is tight and rentals at affordable prices are almost unheard of. It's on the Right Bank."

Marty felt her eyes upon his as if to anticipate his reaction before moving on to Alex. She seemed to take a deep breath before saying, "If you would like to share, you are welcome. We can split the rent three ways. Incidentally, an idea of how long that is liable to be?"

Marty was conflicted. He looked blankly at Alex, which he knew he would interpret as telling him the decision was his.

"The answer is simple: when the money runs out," Alex said. "Depending on how much you charge, it could be, we hope, more than two weeks but no more than a few months, maybe. It would be great." He looked pleased and added, "When do we move in?"

"I'll meet you here tomorrow at 10 in the morning and take you over. You can come simply to inspect and decide accordingly. Or you can check out of your hotel, bring your cases with you and take potluck. Your choice."

"Shall we celebrate over a bit of dinner?" Alex said. "I hear restaurants open about nine and it's almost that now. Marty and I should eat something before we call it a night. Will you join us?"

They ended up with a simple meal in a hole in the wall on the *rue de l'Université*. A charming end to a day of many surprises was Marty's conclusion as they bid Sonia good night. In their hotel room, Marty busied himself with his nightly ablutions and quickly got into bed.

"You haven't said a word since we left Sonia. What's the matter?" Alex said. He turned off the light and stretched out on the twin bed next to Marty's.

"Too much to say, so I say nothing."

"What do you mean?"

"It's late. Too tired to start a long discussion. One example abbreviated should do: How do you know Sonia?"

"I met her at my brother's when I went home for a weekend last year."

Marty decided Alex was being evasive. He knew his brother and he was not an intellectual to have a graduate student as a friend over for dinner. Maybe his wife. But Marty wasn't sure of her either. He had met them once. "Where does Columbia come in?"

"I saw her in New York during Christmas last year. It was at a party by one of the fellows I was talking to about a possible job. A coincidence."

"That's all?

"We also got together for dinner."

"Is she aware of what I am in your life?"

"I doubt it. Why should she even think of it? She only just met you. I like talking to her."

It was not convincing. Marty was uneasy. For him to learn more about how Alex met Sonia was less urgent than dealing with the misgivings he felt of what could happen if they moved into her apartment. There was something about graceful Alex that made all who came in contact with him fall in love. Marty loved him and understood what was attractive about him, although he had never tried to put it into words. Nonetheless, to him it was obvious in the way women sidled up to touch him, to fix his tie, to move the curl that always tumbled over his forehead. He observed this evening the tug that pulled Sonia towards their table in the café and the way she sidled up to him when they walked towards the restaurant. But, he wondered, would she accept that he and Alex were a couple? After what he feared was an interminable interval during which Alex might have fallen asleep he blurted out, "Do you think it's right for two men to move into an apartment with a single woman?"

"Why not?"

"It may look wrong. What happens when she realizes what we are?"

"Stop being silly. This is Paris, Marty, not New York."

"I don't worry about either of us imposing ourselves on her, but you and I, well, our relationship is different. Has she designs on you, do you think?" Marty hid his face in the pillow, waiting for a reaction from Alex.

"Stop talking rot."

"Do we worry about what anyone will say?"

"Why should we care?"

"Well, maybe not—but a threesome, a trio is typically unstable. It can turn into two against one. Maybe not in an unpleasant way, but still…"

"What's wrong with that? Duets sometime, a solo sometimes, a change from simple trios, depending on the mood. Not always the same two or the same one. Is that bad?"

"In principle? No. Practically? Don't know. Haven't tried it. I'm not even sure I want to."

"Why don't we go see the place first? We'll decide after. Now go to sleep."

The next morning Sonia appeared at the appointed time. They treated themselves to a *café au lait* and a *croissant* before a taxi took them across the Seine to the quarter known as the *Marais*, no longer a swamp but a working-class neighborhood. They found themselves in the "real" Paris as they entered a large courtyard enveloped in shadow and guarded by the inevitable dour concierge. Regrettably, it was not the former home of the famous *Mme. de Sévigné,* on the street of the same name, but during that period it probably housed a similar personage, long before it fell upon hard times and was broken up into individual dwellings.

Their steps echoed as they traversed the courtyard and approached the narrow, steep, rickety, dark staircase that led to the apartment. It was enveloped in perpetual darkness broken with the press of a button they probably incorrectly called the *minuterie*.

Metonymy is what it was, the button representing the system that illuminated their path. The clock-like mechanism operated by the button ensured that the dimmest of dim electric lights operated theoretically for a proximate minute but just long enough to enable one to reach the desired landing but not before the key found its way into the keyhole.

At the top of the stairs, after Sonia let them inside the apartment, they entered a long, narrow, dark hallway. To the right, after about ten paces, Sonia opened a door to a smallish room and flicked on the light. It revealed twin beds, a nightstand with an awkward light fixture consisting of what Marty thought had to be a 25-kilowatt bulb and a chair. After another stretch they entered, also to the right, a larger room, empty of furniture except for a folding bridge table and a couple of chairs, which opened into two other rooms. The door to the left led to Sonia's bedroom. The door towards the back opened into a fair-sized room in the middle of which sat a big squat coal stove, the heating center for the apartment. Next to it hulked a bin for coal briquettes and bundles of sticks required to feed it. Centered on the right wall stood a cupboard. Sonia had laid out her empty suitcases against the back wall to form impromptu shelving for magazines, newspapers and other such temporary acquisitions.

Marty was fascinated that the largest room was the least used as living space.

Sonia led them back to the hallway. In the direction of the kitchen the first door opened into the Water Closet. After it came a room just large enough to contain a bathtub and sink. What was that rubber hose hanging into the bathtub from the sink? Marty couldn't resist and ran his hand along the hose from the right-hand faucet to which it was attached to the tub to discover a showerhead resting at the bottom. Holding the showerhead in his hand, he turned to Sonia.

"Simple," she said. "Quirk. One of the ones we have to accept. That's how we shower with warm water. If you want to take a bath, you wait until enough water comes through to fill the tub. If it is not too cold in the room, it may still be hot—warm enough really, if you are lucky, when it is a quarter full. Come, I'll show you the source."

Marty looked at Alex who winked at him. He shrugged. He talked himself into behaving. Don't forget there is no free lunch—no free apartment—take it as an inducement for lower rent—the tradeoff? More time in Paris. He finally managed a smile.

At the end of the hallway, they entered the narrow kitchen, the only room with a window. It faced a shaft. The pantry/cooler was built into the wall under the window. In French it was designated a *garde manger*, the object Sonia took to calling the *mangyguard*, her translation into no known language; it served in place of a would-be-hoped-for refrigerator, or better still in that rather primitive environment, an icebox. Sonia pointed to the tank hanging against the wall angled with the window. It supplied hot water to the sink underneath or the bathroom sink whenever a tap was opened. The bathroom tap was connected to the showerhead imported from the USA.

The tour completed, they returned to the bridge-table room. Sonia turned to Alex for a reaction. He in turn waited for Marty. Marty, oblivious, had wandered away. He had an urge to find a secluded corner in the midst of what, to him, resembled a stage set of multiple doors designed for a farce, each door leading to a windowless room. Sonia had described the rooms as ducks in a row; he saw them more as a labyrinth, albeit minuscule. He found himself in the room with the twin beds. If any, he thought, this would be his preference. He squeezed the mattresses to test for softness. Not too bad. He liked a hard mattress. The night-table lamp needed a good-sized bulb. He liked to read in bed. He and Alex would need another chair. Where to hang clothes? Probably something, he assumed, could be managed between a suitcase and the cupboard in the stove room. How would he and Alex get to either of the components of a regular bathroom? In pajamas? No, probably would need a bathrobe. In any case, they travelled light and had packed neither. In an emergency they put on raincoats. Getting dressed in the middle of the night just to go to the bathroom because of uncontrollable need is a joke.

Marty, what are you doing? clanged in his head. Compromising? He was shocked to hear his voice, as he was alone in the room. But it continued. Do you really want to move in? Thoughtfully considered, the answer was negative. Haven't ever shared with a woman except my mother, of course with father present, and the question right now is do I want to? "Don't know," he muttered as he inched his way out the door, and overheard Alex and Sonia talking shares of rent.

"Sonia, can we come back tomorrow?" Alex said. "I see on Marty's face that he needs to talk. In any case we already paid for tonight at the hotel."

"During the day will be difficult. How about in the evening after seven? We can have a bite together in the neighborhood afterwards—whatever you decide."

Marty and Alex descended the stairs, having to light their way twice because they continued talking at the door after having pushed the light button. "If we move in, we better get a couple of small flashlights to avoid being trapped between light buttons," commented Alex.

Marty grunted.

"You're learning to grunt like an expert. Let's talk instead."

"On the street?"

"How about we stop at a café for a bite."

As they came onto the avenue, they found a bistro and made themselves comfortable at a small table by the wall.

"All right, what's the problem?" Alex said.

"The same one I had last night plus a few others."

"Marty, for heaven's sake, we are not living in Victorian England. There is no problem. This is France. We are not Oscar Wilde facing an obscenity charge. We are in the Paris Oscar Wilde fled to after serving his sentence because of the love that dare not speak its name. Sonia is a sophisticated, or will soon become an even more sophisticated woman, accepting homosexuals and lesbians on the same terms as heterosexuals. To her, we are two friends travelling together. That's how she met us. I can't see what it is that you are turning into a problem."

"Did you notice the way she looked at you yesterday?"

"I guess I did, but you know better than that. You are the one, the only one. That was decided a long time ago. Why bring it up?"

"O.K. But we have nothing but our raincoats."

"What?" Alex shook his head in disbelief. "Come again?"

"O.K. Forget it." Marty contritely switched to a more palatable subject. "What about money? I heard you talking, but all I could figure out is that you were happy."

"Of course, I'm happy. We can stay a couple of months, maybe more, for what we would pay for a couple of weeks for the hotel. Imagine staying long enough to really get a feel of the city. Drink your coffee. When you finish, maybe you will ask for a second cup, after which you will have had enough time to think. I will wait until then to hear your decision."

Marty ate his sandwich and munched on his *cornichon,* slowly, very slowly. He intended to enjoy every morsel of French bread with the butter lathered under the so tasty slice of ham. He was prepared to make the most of it. He wanted as much time as he could drag out to consider the implications of sharing the apartment. He didn't know what he wanted.

Had anything been going on between Alex and Sonia? Could anything develop? He knew Alex; he loved Alex; he didn't want ever to conceive of life without him. Alex, as far as he knew, had never shown interest in a woman, but what did we ever know of another human being? One best knew him in bed, so it is said. Being in bed with Alex was his idea of paradise; he and Alex interchangeable, composites, equal parts of one, of each other. But people change. Could Alex change? He was torn. The if this, if that, if the other discussion with himself came to no conclusion. He gave up when it dawned on him that Alex was delighted with the possibility of extending their stay. If he continued posing obstacles, it might hurt their relationship, and that he couldn't face.

Marty slowly finished his second cup of coffee. Alex jumped when Marty surprised him by the sound of his voice saying, "All right, my dear, we move in."

In no time, they found themselves confronting the concierge. The procedure of getting through the interrogation and up the stairs was easy, although Marty was sure the lady did not omit to give them a looking over, every inch of them. Sonia was there, at the door, to greet them.

"Glad to see you fellows. Proposition too good to turn down?"

"How did you ever guess?" said Alex.

They went into the bridge-table room. The three stood around the table playing a game of who sits where with only two chairs. "We'll have to scrounge for a third chair," said Sonia. "Let me get you the keys so you can bring yourselves over tomorrow. What we better decide now is who moves in where."

Sonia disappeared into her room. Marty and Alex stood until she returned, when Alex motioned for her to sit down. Marty retreated to lean against the wall, giving Alex no choice but to sit facing Sonia. She gave him a set of keys.

"I don't know what you would prefer," Sonia said. "The first room as you come in has twin beds, but we can move one of those beds into this room. We could consider the coal room, but I think it would be too messy to set up." She was sheepish.

Marty stared, unseeing. Was she trying to split us up? Why would she do that? Maybe not, maybe she knows nothing, assumes nothing. She's just a nice girl, an American girl with no preconceived ideas. Marty, please just accept her as you see her until proven otherwise. Funny, special French air filtering for this place has no windows and yet never smells musty. Must be some system, invisible. Good, clean air.

Sonia was still talking—what was she saying? Oh yes, she admitted that whoever takes the middle room would have to contend with her occasionally walking through. It has the only entrance to her room, she reminded them, motioning in the direction of the door behind her. Marty heard Alex ask him if he agreed they leave the twin beds as they were. A sacrifice to his sense of privacy as a so-called unattached single Marty was more than willing to make. He nodded agreement.

Marty could not help but ruminate on what had brought them to Paris. In college shortly after they met, they reacted to their strong attraction by becoming a couple, serene, satisfied, and happy. They could not see living apart and, when they graduated, they thought of San Francisco but New York was just as accommodating to their way of life. They both were confident they could find suitable business opportunities there. When they agreed they wanted to tour Europe as a sort of honeymoon before settling down, they opted first to arrange for living quarters in Manhattan. They searched until they came upon the brownstone on the West Side, an old town house that had been converted into a shared dwelling with two apartments per floor, one facing the front and the other the back. What good fortune brought them were the two studios at the top of the staircase, the third floor, and an unexpected degree of privacy. The price was right and although the rooms were small, they were happy to have their own home.

Alex was fortunate to have gotten the promise of a job at an accounting firm in the fall, but no later than January, prior to tax season. Marty dreamed of running his own bookstore and foresaw no difficulty finding one to work in and learn the business, especially as Alex was prepared to cover their joint expenses as long as necessary. They were content and looked forward to a future together. That future had room for friends, but Marty couldn't conceive of competition.

"If that is settled," Sonia said, "let's talk about..."

"Money?" Alex said smiling as he teased. "I'll bring it tomorrow unless you want it today. I have to go to American Express and cash travelers' checks. You say when."

And so, they became roommates. Marty eventually forgot what they paid. They were forever grateful to the individual who conceived the connection for hot water from the kitchen to the bathtub, even if it was through a sink, so they could shower every day with a supply of hot water on demand. He and Alex learned from Sonia not only how to keep the coal stove alive but also how to feed the *mangyguard* by shopping in a strange language in a series of small shops where they were welcomed as if they belonged. They indeed even willingly cleaned floors on hands and knees if the occasion demanded. The art of politely squabbling and making up became endemic in the household.

Marty eventually convinced himself that luck found them at the *Deux Magots,* guided them to an apartment, and allowed them to live like regular citizens in the city of their dreams.

But he remained uneasy about the possibility of encountering Sonia at night. His recurring nightmare was of a naked man, either with his face or Alex's, bumping unexpectedly into Sonia in the dark. And yet he knew there was no question of a naked Alex going anywhere. Simultaneously he worried about her. Was she simply naïve? Was she in denial about him and Alex? He couldn't decide. He was fortunate never to have felt rejected. What would she feel though if and when she eventually understood Alex would not, could not, respond to her? He tried to imagine her hurt. Stop transferring, Marty, he scolded himself, just because you find Alex irresistible you are convinced everyone similarly reacts.

* * * * *

On their first Sunday Sonia suggested they go to the *Marché aux Puces,* the renowned market whose name projects an image of a sea of fleas and which, since its genesis, has had its name filched by many an imitator worldwide. Alex and Marty followed Sonia on a short walk to the *Place de la Bastille,* not to the nearest *Métro* station but the closest in the direct line to their destination. They purchased tickets and made their way to the correct underground platform to await the train to take them on their first extended journey within the city. The second-class coach brought them to the *Porte de Clignancourt*. They emerged on the avenue of the same name to be faced by a vast open space, a picturesque labyrinth of stalls, a sort of permanent fair. Among antiques and other bric-a-brac, they were promised chairs at give-away-prices.

As they meandered, they came upon a stall with new and used clothing. Marty stopped and exclaimed, "Alex and I need pajamas." They huddled and a dictionary emerged. The search produced the closest equivalent to be clothing for the night. Sonia, the most fluent in French, was given the task to negotiate. She asked for *vêtements de nuit*—no, not small, large, for these two gentlemen. Marty was overjoyed he and Alex had not gotten themselves to a department store, for this was more fun. For the equivalent of about $5, Marty became the proud possessor of a Popsicle-orange garment suitable for Halloween and Alex of a black and white pants-and-jacket set in huge alternating diamonds reminiscent of the costume worn by the Harlequin character in Italian *commedia dell'arte*. Marty caught Alex's eye letting him know how small a dent their purchase made on their funds and consequently advising him to ignore the fancy-ball aspect of their acquisitions. Marty promised himself never to wear the togs beyond the walls of the Paris apartment.

On their hunt for chairs, the main object of their expedition, Marty got lost among books as Alex wandered over to old paintings while Sonia tugged at both of them in what Marty presumed was the right direction. When they finally hit upon straight-back, wooden chairs they almost danced a jig. Each picked a chair, inspected it, sat on it, and if judged sturdy, set it aside. Decisions, decisions, two chairs or three. They eventually settled on three, one for the bridge-table room, one for the twin-bedded room plus one, at Sonia's suggestion, for the coal room.

Alex gave Sonia the equivalent of the $7. She took it absentmindedly. "How do you split $7 by three?" she asked.

To Marty the question was unsettling, because he had no doubt she could do the math. Although he told himself he could joke about the way the cost of the chairs unwittingly converted into an odd number, he kept quiet. To fill the silence, Marty said to Alex, "Accountant, use your professional expertise."

Marty paid no attention to what Alex replied. His mind galloped. But was Sonia aware that when he was with Alex he generally carried almost no money? Did she note that Alex without being prompted paid for both their pajamas? Did she take it for granted they would privately sort out who owed what? In any case, Marty reminded himself that women who travel together might also have a kitty, a sort of cash fund for joint expenses. So, could Sonia not assume they had a similar arrangement? The main thing, yes, was that they had to be careful to conceal any outward expression of their intimacy when they were together. And yet, he was confident that by this time they were good enough actors to carry it off. And even good actors sometimes forget their lines. And ...

All at once Marty was holding the bigger chair, which Alex had thrust into his hands, and his attention was diverted to the problem of taking the awkward object home. Sonia picked up the smallest and Alex was left with the third. Marty was pleased there was no time for her to quibble over her share; she could take it up later with Alex, who would tell her to forget it, for he and Marty had agreed they would absorb their common expenses.

The return home posed no obstacle. The trains were relatively empty, inching towards noon, and gave them enough room to maneuver through turnstiles, up and down stairs, and into coaches. After a change at *La Bastille*, they emerged on the *rue Saint Antoine*, a few short blocks from home, proud possessors of chairs and sleepwear.

Alex started singing, "I'll be loving you always..." a popular tune. Marty joined him. Sonia followed, but not having yet practiced together, was a bit out of tune. Their newly formed trio needed more work.

* * * * *

The following Sunday, a blaze of sunlight greeted the city. An occasional gift from the heavens that aroused the citizenry to rush outdoors under rarely beheld blue skies. Marty learned of the turn the weather had taken when Sonia returned bearing fresh *croissants* for breakfast. His shout announcing the news caught Alex taking a shower. Although he had an inkling of the bounty being offered, he was not yet sufficiently Parisian to gather the group to run into the sunny street at first notice. He wanted his *croissant* first.

One of their new chairs graced the two already in existence to create a dining/living room in the center of the maze. Alex devised an upended suitcase set next to the table, covered with a napkin, as a so-to-speak sideboard on which to place the food from the kitchen. By magic sufficient dishes had appeared to meet their needs. The morning vanished as *croissants* were devoured between coffees gulped on the run. For lunch, Alex wanted some fresh bread. He decided to go down to the the *rue Saint Antoine* to buy cheese, butter, olives and tomatoes and whatever else would appeal. Marty meanwhile made another pot of coffee.

They finally sat down at the table and, to be sure, with the *Paris Herald Tribune* at hand. Attention focused on food. Voices emerged from sections of the paper held up as shields. "This can't be a conversation among adults," muttered Marty as he peeked behind the news section in his hand. Echoes of pass this or pass that and what did you say and what do you want reverberated. He thought again and wondered how it is that a familial pattern can be established among strangers in a few short days. Count them, he told himself, not much more than two weeks. He laughed aloud.

"What was that all about?" Alex said.

"Something caught in my throat," Marty answered.

And thus, Sunday became the favored day for the trio to spend time together. Saturday generally was Sonia's library day, if no other work intervened. She was busy Monday through Friday at school or locating sources to research or interview. Alex and Marty followed a loose schedule devised according to the French *Guides Bleus - Paris,* which they faithfully followed every day of the week except Sunday.

When they finally emerged in the courtyard, having dawdled into afternoon, they were greeted by dim light. The sun had vanished. They looked up at the typically overcast sky from which a gentle drizzle came down to engulf them, so light it made for clamminess but not dense enough to dampen spirits. It was sufficient in and of itself that when darkness came it would convert the streets into reflecting pools for the lights beaming down from the amazing collection of street lamps in the city. No matter, they were already wearing their raincoats. Perennially optimistic Sonia had her camera.

They turned towards the *Place des Vosges*, the jewel of the neighborhood. It had previously been known as the *Place Royale*. Its uniform set of hewn-stone and brick structures had originally been designed to house silk manufacturers, but in the days of Louis XIV the structures were converted into dwellings for the aristocracy. They wandered off in different directions. Marty could imagine Sonia trying to discover which apartment had been Victor Hugo's home. He preferred to see himself attending one of the ladies of the court rather than haggling over silk. On second thought, it occurred to him that as a middle-class character he might have a better chance of being admitted on equal terms if he were a silk merchant. What Alex could be dreaming up he ventured not to guess.

They found themselves in what had been designed as a perfect square surrounded by a series of street-level galleries. They had read in the guidebook that its character had not changed since the days of Henry IV. A fountain in each corner of the garden with the statue of Louis XII in the center, they were informed, made for pleasing symmetry.

When Marty stopped to inspect the statue of Louis, Alex approached him and asked, "Why is symmetry pleasing?"

"Are you kidding? Are you trying to bring us back into the present, are you? And I was dreaming of being a silk merchant." Alex, no surprise to Marty, was in the present devising an intellectual puzzle to occupy him.

Sonia caught up with them. She took Alex by the arm and said, "Why should it not be?"

"Well, let's see," Alex said as if ruminating aloud. "I can think of the Japanese potter working on his wheel deliberately creating imperfection because, in his eyes, natural beauty is never as faultless as what his wheel will produce." He paused to look around. "What else? I also heard somewhere that Persian weavers made sure to weave a flaw into the design of a carpet. Perfection in design is what, bad luck? Only the deity is perfect. I don't know; I remember so many of their carpets as being perfectly symmetrical, except for the jolt of a break in configuration. It is invisible unless you know where to look."

"If you don't know, why bring it up?" Marty said. "But what are you talking about? Does symmetry imply perfection? Is that it?"

"Well, take painting," Alex continued, oblivious of the question. "We like what is off center, when the proportions are right. I, for one, find that more pleasing. Balance yes, but not necessarily symmetry. Is it architecture that accommodates symmetry better? Sometimes, not always. I don't know."

Sonia faced Alex. She said, "It is thought in certain quarters that symmetry is the essence of human beauty. Depends on what period you're talking about. Sixteenth, seventeenth century France aimed for symmetry. I think imported from Italy. The idea of the *piazza*. Hence the square where you are now standing. Asymmetry was fashionable at times, symmetry at others. The Greeks aiming for harmony came up with a formula, a golden mean, to define the right proportions, for example, in paintings. So did others later."

Marty stepped away. He had enough of symmetry and tuned it out. As he surveyed the scene, Alex saying he liked to talk to Sonia reverberated. Alex had an inquisitive, undisciplined mind that responded to any subject he chanced upon. What had originally attracted Marty to him was his incredible range of knowledge. But, here he had evidence that Sonia was not only insatiably curious but also similarly erudite. He suddenly understood how their curiosities could feed on each other. Nothing one could object to, could one, Marty, wondered. No, but let's hope that's all it is.

"Can't you feel something special here?" Marty said. He wanted to break up the unending talk.

"Except the garden, its wrought-iron railing around it—what makes up the *piazza*—it could be in better condition," said Alex.

'That's a different matter," Marty countered. "That's a problem of maintenance. Can't we just agree the place is beautiful, like an old lady who needs better makeup and repair of her quoins and some window dressing?"

"Bravo," Sonia said. "If we want to continue our discussion based on vague knowledge, let's wander over to the *Louvre*. There we can consider the problems of an art, like painting, that aims to suggest illusion on a flat surface and whether what we can observe and reproduce should be symmetrical or not, whether it achieves the right proportion, reflects imperfect nature or aims for the ideal. If we hurry, we might still get there before it closes."

"I just asked a simple question—one question," Alex said. He made a face as if he were hurt.

Sonia took Alex by the hand and admonished him. "Ask, my child. Keep on searching for answers and you shall become wise." She smiled up at him and, teasing, added, "Even if none of us can give you an answer."

Alex hugged her and slowly turned away to face the fountain. He threw up his hands. Marty sensed a peacefulness of spirit enveloping them. He wondered if it was because they were the only ones whose voices resounded in the empty square. Eventually they gathered again without a word and cut towards the river and followed the Seine until they could cross over to the Louvre.

On Sunday admission was free. It was approaching closing time, and they rushed to the galleries. When they came to the stairs, Marty looked up and was struck by the *Winged Victory of Samothrace* perched on a pedestal at the top. She appeared to be flying over him. He froze.

Alex and Sonia were halfway up when they missed him. Marty heard Sonia calling him, but he motioned for them to come back down. He said, "What's the matter with you? Don't you look? This absolutely gorgeous female—is she perfectly symmetrical, Alex?"

"No human being is perfectly symmetrical," Alex said.

"Give me one more minute to delight in her." Marty stood immobile. "I've fallen in love with her," he said.

Sonia started up again while Alex waited for Marty. When Marty came up to him, in a whisper, Alex said, "If you carry on like this, I'll be jealous."

"Wasted emotion." Marty smirked. "She's marble; you're flesh."

They passed through the hall with the frescos, the Italian primitives and finally reached the Grand Gallery. As they spread out, the announcement came through that it was closing time.

When they emerged on the *Place du Carousel*, they walked over to the *Pont du Carrousel* to cross over to the Left Bank. On the embankment, by the bookstalls, they turned towards the *Place Saint Michel*.

They walked arm-in-arm along the quay, Sonia between Alex and Marty, the three of them in lock step occasionally snaking along the narrow sidewalk crowded with Sunday strollers. Suddenly the sky opened and patches of blue appeared as the sun began its descent into the horizon. Sonia became more and more entranced with the sky. She grabbed her camera and began to hover around like a butterfly looking for a comfortable perch from which to take a photograph. She searched for a good angle to capture the Magritte-like clouds. At times she would disappear among the crowd on a bridge, put the camera down on the bridgehead, bend down to look through the lens, study the image, manipulate the dials, look again and eventually move on. Alex and Marty never stopped, merely slowing their pace when they lost sight of her.

Sonia, when she rejoined them, grabbed Alex by the arm. She said, "Come over here, both of you. Let me take your picture."

"You want us by the bridge?"

"Yes, the idea is the sky. You're accidental."

As soon as Sonia finished taking her shot, Alex said, "Marty, don't move." He rushed up to Sonia and asked, "Can't we have one of the three of us? Maybe we could ask a nice anyone passing by to take it for us? You can set it up."

Sonia turned to ask the first person who approached. She aimed the camera at Marty who stood against the parapet and adjusted the focus and the light. Alex again joined Marty, and they coaxed Sonia to get between them, in front. Their photographer approved. They resumed their walk, the three again arm-in-arm.

At the *Pont Neuf* Sonia disappeared. The sun was descending, and she frantically moved about to capture the moment. Marty and Alex leaned over the parapet, concentrating on the river below, while they waited for her.

Marty momentarily thought himself in New York. Maybe it was the sight of moving water that brought to mind the perch from the Brooklyn Bridge he discovered on one of his walks during the summer after they moved into their studios. He and Alex had then planned an evening of dancing—with each other—when they got to Paris. At home it was an activity construed as a violation of the moral code. He knew of bars where men did indeed dance together, but neither he nor Alex willingly patronized them. But in Paris, a liberated Paris, he had heard it was publicly accepted in certain quarters. He and Alex already had figured out that the little street with *boîtes* where they could dance was walking distance from the apartment, not far from the *Place de la Bastille*. Marty realized he was being selfish: he wanted to be alone with Alex on a dance floor, or, at least, feel as if he were alone. He didn't want Sonia, or any other female who knew them, there. Maybe it was a place where she might want to go slumming, but not with me, Marty repeated over and over. I won't be comfortable with a woman in such a place, not this kind of woman. I want to go dancing, dancing with Alex, dancing now, today, not tomorrow, tonight.

"We've been together all day. It's not like days when we don't see Sonia until dinner, if then. Don't you think maybe she'll be tired of chasing sky and be just as glad to put her feet up? We can take off and hope she won't feel abandoned."

"True. But what about dinner? Shouldn't we plan to go somewhere together?"

Marty and Alex stopped short as Sonia caught them unawares. "What's the matter with you two? It's the most exquisite sunset and you seem to be off somewhere, ignoring the present, using your smallest voice so I can't hear a word. Come admire."

"Yes, it's a pure Parisian apparition," Marty said, trying unsuccessfully to be funny and tongue-twisty alliterative.

"Come help me set up the camera. I should have the tripod. It needs a timed exposure." She searched for a flat surface, but none satisfied her. "Look at it! Have you ever seen such an array of colors: red, purple, pink, ochre and surrounding shades from white to dark gray that could have been painted by an artist? And such interesting shapes."

As she spoke the sky began the transition from dusk to night, and her film speed even with a timed exposure could hardly capture the scene. Marty said, "Too late, Sonia. Just imprint it in memory."

"Come with me. Let's set it up on the parapet. It's worth a try. You hold it. I'll set the shutter speed. Maybe something will still come out."

After Sonia finished fiddling with the dials, she took Marty's finger and put it on the camera. He held it down as hard as he could to keep the case from jumping when she pressed the shutter release. He uttered a quiet plea to the god of photography not to let her fail.

"What were you two mumbling about?" Sonia asked as they walked on. "I couldn't hear what you were saying."

"We are contemplating a bite to eat," Alex said.

Marty felt something like shame overcome him. How could they ever tell her they had been plotting to evade her while she was plotting camera angles? Not ever and remain friends, until—yes, until, he was convinced she accepted that he and Alex were bound together. Only then could they be completely open with each other. Yes, let's hope it comes about, soon.

"Why so early? You know restaurants open at nine. Not too long to wait," Sonia said, her voice rising in frustration.

"I'm a bit hungry, that's why. Maybe an appetizer. Would you mind?" Alex asked in his gentlest voice.

"Men," Sonia said. "We haven't eaten since brunch. Funny, I'm not hungry."

They crossed over to the Right Bank and found a café. They sat down on the terrace and ordered sandwiches. Marty sensed Sonia was annoyed. He couldn't blame her but accepted he needed to feel guilty.

"How about a drink, Sonia?" Marty said.

"I think I'll have a beer. Let's pretend it is sort of tea time, high beer time, with which it is appropriate to eat little sandwiches." She smiled a devilish smile and added, "Lots of fortified liquid will be useful to wash it down—

even if I do love salami and cheese on a baguette instead of dinner."

The waiter took their order. Alex took on the guise of an angel. Sonia stared at the street.

After the waiter put down plates and drinks, each one politely waited for the other to start. Sonia grabbed a cornichon. Alex and Marty picked at their baguettes while Sonia munched on her pickle. When she finished her sandwich, Sonia picked herself up and said, "See you later, folks." She walked in the direction of the apartment.

Alex and Marty ordered coffee. "No need to tell stories," Alex said. "We'll probably be back early enough to bid her good night or late enough for her to know only what she needs to know—better still, no more than she may want to know. Tomorrow is another day." Alex took a deep breath. "I would hate to hurt her. She's too good a human being for that."

"Let's bring her some flowers, a peace offering. Tomorrow," Marty said.

* * * * *

Marty and Alex drank one coffee slowly and another even more slowly, before they started to walk, or rather drag, up the r*ue de Rivoli* until it became the *rue Saint Antoine* and they came upon the *Place de la Bastille*. As they came upon the square, their courage almost failed; they did not want to be early and had no idea how to delay. Marty looked at his watch and noted it was after nine. But they plodded on and had no trouble finding the *rue de Lappe*. It was the first narrow street they came upon. It was crammed with establishments that seemed to meet their wish. They had no way to judge among them. They aimed to get there before drinks if not drugs overcame the habitués, or so they imagined. And they did. All they wanted was to dance.

Marty was overwhelmed by the smell of alcohol and the acrid smell of sweaty bodies redolent of cheap perfume when he entered the smoked-filled room. He wasn't sure if what he expected was a combo of tired musicians playing either a foxtrot or a tango, but what he heard was neither. The dance floor was supposed to be filled with louche men, sailors dancing with pudgy boys wearing heavy make-up, older women with dyed hair and young girls in short skirts, drugged types of every sex. He had somehow convinced himself that the men had to wear kerchiefs around their necks and caps on their heads. It was supposed to be a sordid scene redolent of the post-1929, Wall-Street-crash era he remembered reading about in one of Somerset Maugham's novels. It was close, but no sailors and no saxophone. It would do. They would dance.

"I've heard better," Alex said. "But the accordion player is not bad."

"I don't care. I want you—with your arms around me."

At a table for two, Alex ordered Cognac. As the alcohol infused his brain, Marty imagined himself sitting in the bar Maugham had described as he remembered it. He was on that dance floor dancing among the boys with made-up eyes, dancing with men with caps on and handkerchiefs round their necks and the girls with short dresses dancing with gaunt women. He was in their midst with Alex, with a shorter Alex, Alex in a tight dress, a plunging neckline. It was a gaudy, cheap dress a streetwalker might wear, stamped with a profusion of red wild flowers. But to him,

Alexandra was a beautiful, desirable object. Her cleavage although barely noticeable—she was flat chested—was so inviting he could hardly restrain an urge to tear the dress off. In apache dancing, he assumed, it might be acceptable to attempt to do so. No, he had dreamed of dancing for so long, he wasn't going to let an unrestrained impulse get the better of him, not yet. Because the head of Alexandra came up to his shoulder, he could at least gape down the neckline as it flapped open when he twirled her and so satisfied his desire for naked flesh. At moments he wondered if he had wandered far afield becoming so fixated on Alexandra, for he only really wanted Alex. It was the tango, he reminded himself, that was the cause; maybe men danced tango with men, but he had never heard of it—and he wanted badly to dance a tango with Alex or Alexandra—he didn't care.

Marty forced himself to concentrate. He was dancing to the Argentinean tango, *Caminito*. He remembered it as the story of a lover come to bid farewell for the last time to the narrow lane, the *caminito*, covered with clover and flowering rush, erased by time, where he and his lover once met. He could almost feel his hand on Alexandra's spine leading her into a forward walk, heel first, foot flat, one, two, three, four, feet together, turn, slide, slink, swivel, backward walk, dip, take the hand, hold at hip level, move away, swivel. Count of eight. Dance. Ecstasy.

"Shall we order another Cognac or shall we dance first?" Alex said.

Marty, confronting reality discovered, he was sitting next to Alex. "Are you all right?" Alex asked. "You have a funny look on your face. Are you feeling faint or something?"

"I'm fine. I was just sort of daydreaming you and I were dancing the tango, you in a sexy dress..."

"In drag?" Alex interrupted. "Should we try it sometime?"

"Let's dance."

Marty rose slowly to follow Alex onto the dance floor. Marty gazed at Alex with love oozing out of his pores. If Alex misunderstood why Marty clung to him tightly, Marty was not inclined to explain he was still under the influence of his frenzied infusion of tango sexuality. Marty loved the feel of swaying in rhythm with Alex's body as if they were one.

"I like these French ballads, don't you?" Alex said.

"Yes, I do, too, the melodies, the rhythm. But I wish they were about our kind of love."

Alex hummed along with the music. It was a popular song. It was about a life in rose, not the flower but the color pink, a happy life. Alex whispered made-up words of the French song in English. "When I hold you in my arms, I think I'm hearing Brahms," he mouthed,

"And I see the world all rosy. He talks to me of love, the adoring words of my very own dove, and says to me something ...of trala la la lala." Marty was moved. He was in his arms, basking in his warmth, his head against Alex's head. It was pure bliss.

When the music stopped, they returned to their table and ordered another Cognac. They held hands. They watched the other dancers: women danced with girls, men danced with boys, men danced with women. Marty and Alex joined them on the dance floor. Once, they were asked to dance by striking looking women, if one disregarded the heavy hand with which makeup had been applied and the threadbare clothing—or were they men in drag? Although flattered, they refused. They shook their heads, smiled, shrugged, raised their hands in the French manner, to intimate they just wanted to dance with each other. They had heard of apache dancing and expected to see some examples, but no couple on the dance floor fought or pretended to fight. They saw no woman fighting her pimp or her lover, while he slapped her, threw her or pulled her hair. Some of them did appear to be capable of roughhouse in a tense environment and could have been dangerous. Perhaps it was. Somehow apache dancing, after it was appropriated by the French upper classes from the underworld, traveled to Argentina and subsequently returned transformed as the tango. But they heard no tango—only French waltz, two-step, fox trot. Alex and Marty were right to get there early, as the atmosphere became increasingly contentious as the evening progressed.

At a little after midnight with Alex slightly drunk, Marty not quite sober but with aching feet and both contentedly exhausted, they agreed it was time to settle the bill. The sound of their footsteps echoing in the deserted streets followed them home. They climbed the stairs to the apartment quietly and tiptoed into their room. As they kissed goodnight, Marty was pleased to have confirmation Alex was as glad as he that they had fulfilled one of their dreams—to dance with each other, in public.

That morning before Marty and Alex started on their round of sightseeing they arranged a bouquet of roses at the foot of the door to Sonia's room. The note perched against an impromptu vase read, "We love you *beaucoup*." It was signed A. and M.

* * * * *

Marty and Alex waited for Sonia to come home dawdling over cocktail-hour wine seated around the center of their French home. When she eventually sauntered in, she pecked each three times in the French manner before disappearing into her bedroom. Emerging in jeans, she plunked herself into a chair, poured herself a glass of wine, took a sip and, after what seemed like forever, casually said, "I need an escort this coming Thursday night." She took another sip and fixing her eyes on Alex, added, "Alex, dear, can we abandon Marty for an evening?"

She leaned back, her legs stretched out in front of her. To Marty she was the picture of a relaxed, confident human being, expecting nothing but acquiescence, blatantly assuming he would accede to her having Alex to herself for an evening. Screw you was his unspoken retort. "Have you decided yet?" she said.

Alex, having risen from the table, leaned against the wall and assumed the pose of man willing to swallow bait. "What's the lure?" he said.

"I have two tickets to the opera."

"Taunting. What opera?"

"'Tristan und Isolde.' It's billed as Kirsten Flagstad's farewell performance and is sold out. Enough?"

"That's Wagner?"

Marty knew Alex was being coy. To hear a performance of Tristan with Flagstad was a unique opportunity. He couldn't hold it against him if he accepted. However, this opera was special; it was theirs, his and

Alex's alone, something precious. How could Alex dare to listen to the love-death scene without him? How could he ignore that they had spent most of their college years listening together to the recording with Flagstad and Melchior at the end of every day before dinner? It was theirs alone and, according to his lights, not to be shared with anyone else and certainly not with a woman. Was he alone in feeling this way? Was he being unnecessarily sensitive? He steeled himself to hear what Alex would decide.

"Yes, of course," Sonia said. She looked at Alex, her eyes trying to divine if he were serious. She must have taken his question on its merits and proceeded to a lengthy exposition. Marty half heard something about German composer—his own libretto—a mediaeval romance—a love potion—a Knight of the Round Table and the daughter of the king of Ireland—ending in a glorious paean to love and death. Marty couldn't help but admire her patience as he heard her admonish Alex that he had to have known it, for it was a classic myth. Little could she be aware that he probably knew both the story and the music as well as, if not better than, she did.

Marty heard Alex ask, "Do I dare ask how much the tickets are?"

"Let that be a surprise," Sonia said. "But if the seats are up in the gods will you be disappointed?"

"Not if the price is right. I suppose French gods are no different than English or American gods."

"Correct. Like all gods they are in the heavens. Good view of midgets; superb acoustics."

Alex let out a guffaw. Sonia turned to Marty, "Can we buy you a ticket to a movie?"

"No thanks. I'll figure something out. I'm a big boy, you know." Marty would never admit he was, on reflection, glad he was not the escort. The few times he had had occasion to go to the opera he had been miserable. He did not enjoy sitting in narrow seats in the dark for hours in the highest reaches of an opera house with his legs cramped under him. He preferred to listen to music at home if he could not afford seats with legroom. Alex, on the other hand, seemed to manage, and never missed a chance to hear a live performance. Wagner, this particular Wagner, was a different story. If he were a cat, he would growl in distress.

Marty examined Alex and Sonia, who seemed content to have reached agreement, although probably with no more satisfaction than if they had crossed safely a late-afternoon, jam-packed street against traffic. No need to fuss, he told himself. When she asked the question, he couldn't decide what Sonia intended. He often thought she couldn't be as naïve as she appeared, but then he would doubt his judgment. He was convinced Alex was not averse to letting himself be loved—none of us are—but he was blind, or believed he should be, to the kind of love he could not, should not, reciprocate. He prayed it was not sexual desire that drove Sonia. Marty was tempted by the idea that if anything it was a matter of two minds playing off each other, call it intellectual attraction. But how blind was she to his relationship with Alex? He couldn't figure her out. He just liked her—most of the time.

"Tickets were hard to get," Sonia said. "It sold out almost immediately."

Marty tried to hold his tongue but couldn't resist. "But how did you manage?"

"I scrounged."

"I read there were long lines. A civilized mob scene with people standing for hours, some all night. I didn't know you indulged."

Sonia winked at Alex. "All right, I'll tell you. An acquaintance at school bought two tickets. Can't use them. If I would have stood in line, I could have bought three, couldn't I? But what is the source of such gossip?"

"Some of us manage to read a newspaper." Marty couldn't help putting in a dig. He guessed Sonia might be reading *Le Monde* or *Le Figaro* at school, but he had never seen her bring one home. He continued, "An easy way to pick up information. But thanks. I'm glad you have tickets. You'll enjoy it more than I would."

If Marty sounded sarcastic, he didn't mean it. He wanted to believe. And yet he had the impression that French students warded off foreigners as a matter of course. The environment was not open, friendly, not like at an American school. Maybe it was the bourgeois class-consciousness of the French that made them so mistrustful of the foreigner; maybe it was their history of German occupation. He was convinced she had made nothing more than a chance acquaintance if that. Besides which, he couldn't imagine anybody going to the trouble of buying tickets so sought after and then discovering a conflict in dates. He had a strong sense Sonia had to have worked on her thesis not to waste time and survive the long wait in line. Besides which, she was undoubtedly fibbing, as only two tickets were sold to a customer. If Alex was accepting, it was not his place to mumble unpleasantly. It had to be the truth. Marty let it go.

Marty and Alex on the morrow decided to inspect the opera house. Alex was curious to preview what awaited him. They took the *Métro* to the *Avenue de l'Opéra* and emerged to face the sumptuous new-baroque structure. To their surprise, they learned it had officially opened only in 1875 and been restored and modernized in 1936. The architect, who lent his name to the building, was one Charles Garnier, although at the time it was commonly known simply as "The Opera." They walked around and admired the outside of the structure embellished with statuary of all kinds, a sort of embarrassment of riches.

Marty stopped and uttered the first words since morning. "In its ugliness, it's beautiful."

"I count seven arcades at the end of the flight of steps through which one enters," Alex said. "But I still see the building somewhat symmetrically with the huge dome at the top, don't you agree?"

"Why not an even number?"

"Marty, you aren't saying much. What's wrong?"

"Nothing."

"I don't believe you. Is it Tristan?"

"Maybe."

"I know what you are thinking. It is our music, always ours. No way can Sonia compete. None. I want that inscribed in your skull. Remember. I will accompany Sonia, such a great opportunity, but it is purely a social exercise. I am practicing. You should practice. We'll take turns. We need to learn to cover. We have a chance with a charming lady. When I start work and I need a partner, a female partner, when we can't appear together socially, it will be good to have an established relationship so I can ask without asking too much. I'll hear the music on

Thursday and imagine I am hearing it for both of us. We both like her, don't we?"

"Yes."

"Is it that you don't trust me?"

"No."

"You know that I love you more than I will ever love anyone else."

"Yes."

"I have an idea. Tristan is hopeless—a one-time affair. Why don't we go around to the box office and see what's available? Let's buy three tickets to something so you can at least see the house. I mean the grand staircase. The guidebook says it is something special, grandiose. Let's go look. You can surely spend one evening suffering and not complain. Maybe we'll be lucky and find you an aisle seat."

Marty was aware Alex was coaxing; he squirmed. "O.K.," he said.

"You are overwhelming me with a bout of logorrhea."

Marty ignored Alex and his sarcasm and went up to a poster advertising an unfamiliar Honegger opera. It was *Joan of Arc at the Stake* and seemed to be a one-act to be followed by a second act ballet entertainment. He was intrigued and tugged at Alex to come take a look. Alex intimated it was probably written before the war but infrequently performed. He didn't know much about it or him, but suggested they see if there were tickets. They walked up to the box office to look at the price list. "First, before you buy, are you sure we can spend this kind of money?" Marty said.

"No need to worry. We spend little."

"Come to think of it, we may only get half the value. I read somewhere something about the ballet company not being very good. We may want to leave at intermission."

"Are you asking, in advance, for permission to leave at intermission? Why not consider reversing course and saving your inestimable words for something worthwhile?" Alex grinned, suggesting he was only teasing.

"I'll take it under advisement." Marty grinned back.

After they purchased tickets, they decided not to visit the Opera's library, the only section open to the public, and went up to *Montmartre*. It was a sunny day and a good opportunity to mosey around. At the *Place du Tertre* they rested their feet in an outdoor café and basked in the sun.

"I'm still thinking of the carpet weavers," Alex said. "Could one say that according to their tradition a mortal cannot aim for perfection, for only God—that is, Allah—is perfect? I seem to remember having heard that once." He was pensive.

"Where were we? Oh yes, in the *Place des Vosges* discussing art. All right, we'll gnaw that bone again." Marty benevolently worked on his face so as to appear to be seriously considering the subject. "Little me, hard as I try, every time I think I have finished a task perfectly, I discover a mistake. So, I guess we may be better off deliberately making a mistake. We will know where it is, and he who allows us to make mistakes because we are human will not have to make us make another. Maybe the same goes for carpet weavers."

"The idea of a perfect deity is imbued in all religions," Alex went on as if he hadn't heard a word. "The corollary seems to be that what is on earth has to be imperfect so as not to compete."

"Interesting thought. But there are some things on earth that are perfect. Can we, say, argue with a perfect flower?" Marty figured he better not be impertinent: Alex was serious. Odd the subjects that would attract his attention from which he would not stray.

"Maybe we are only allowed certain perfection."

"I don't follow you. Perfection and symmetry are not the same thing, or are they? We did start with the notion of symmetry, didn't we?"

"Guess you're right, as always, Marty, my dear. We'll look into it sometime, whenever that shall be. If I add, 'If not now, when' we'll end up nowhere. Let's enjoy this last stretch of irresponsible time—how's that for phrase making—in the here and now, in this lovely square."

Because Wagner operas are long and usually start early, Marty fixed a quick bite in late afternoon for Sonia and Alex that Thursday. While they dressed, he sat at table, nibbling leftovers. When Sonia emerged from her room, she was as lovely as Cinderella dressed for the ball. A pale blue silk sheath set off her golden hair as it fell in soft waves in a pageboy over her shoulders. The scent of perfume, musky and rich, was a perfect complement. She shimmered.

To Marty her eyes spoke a familiar language. They sparkled with more than delight and anticipation. He recalled the first time he and Alex had gone for a long walk outside of campus when they were in college. They had entered a quiet forested glen where they could be alone. And he remembered the tension that crept over his body, the tension produced by an uncontrollable urge to appease the love he felt for Alex, a physical urge to possess him, as strong as—if not stronger than—hunger. It radiated from his eyes. He was conscious he was complementing what Alex was projecting. Sonia's gaze radiated that same desire. He felt like an intruder. He restrained any reaction, for he comforted himself with the knowledge that it takes two to consummate a love. He uttered a quiet prayer that Alex remember that his role was to be the friendly escort the occasion demanded so that she, on a future occasion, would similarly reciprocate.

Alex was ready. His blond forelock, as always, fell softly over his forehead, and Marty could not help but attest he was a handsome, attractive man, a worthy counterpart for the evening to the lady waiting to be taken to the carriage that would deliver them to their fairy-tale opera. But Alex, Marty repeated to himself, was merely her escort, not her prince.

If Marty was envious, it was because of the opera, not because Alex was accompanying Sonia. One was the consequence of the other, so he decided he could not be envious of either. They were three friends sharing an apartment, he told himself. They had to learn to split, say, as a pair and a single, not always the same pair nor the same single. The little group had to be capable of turning into its various configurations, didn't it? This night Alex and Sonia were going to play a duet inspired by Wagner. Marty could hear the two of them playing a fourhanded piano transcription of the short melody to which the shepherd boy switches to let the dying Tristan know Isolde has arrived. He could not vouch that such a transcription existed. No matter. They couldn't be playing the "*Liebestod*;" Alex wouldn't permit it, Marty was certain. That was his and Marty's, theirs alone, not to be shared. Marty was off on his own, making awful noises on a clarinet he did not know how to play. He was just blowing air. But he had to learn to play solo better before the next time, didn't he?

* * * * *

After Marty fetched a taxi for them and sent them on their way, he decided to go for a stroll along the Seine. But first he cleared the kitchen clutter; he had to satisfy the urge to have everything around him neat and in order. When he eventually emerged from the courtyard, the *rue de Sevigné* greeted him in the dim light characteristic of a side street after dark. He was not tempted to linger, for spooks might hover around the corner, if not Inspector Javert searching for his quarry. He walked quickly to the *rue de Rivoli* and stopped to admire the *Hôtel de Ville*, the city hall, when he reached its square. Marty then followed the embankment to cross over the right arm of the Seine to reach the *Cathédral de Notre Dame* on the *Ile de la Cité*. He entered the holy precinct to rest for a while and savor the silence. In his daydream he was present at Napoleon's coronation until the reverberations of the organ broke into his reverie. If it was for his benefit, he could only be grateful that the organist decided to practice at this hour. He recognized the beginning of the "Great Fantasia and Fugue in G minor." Yes, it was Bach. It was the monumental fantasy. The regular beat held him captive. He felt his whole body relax as he concentrated on the waves of sound as they floated up and down restrained by a pedal point that flowed at a consistent pace until it came to rest. He was overcome with a sense of harmony and wellbeing. He leaned against the back of the pew and rested his head. He felt himself being propelled upwards, along the slender columns of the nave. The spatial rhythm matched the music, which reverberated and enveloped him in a cocoon. He was transported by the currents of sound into a mystical realm, at peace with himself, at peace with the world.

When silence returned, Marty wandered out and took the *Petit Pont* to cross over the other arm of the Seine to reach the *Quai Saint Michel*. He had reached the Left Bank and the heart of the student quarter, but he decided not to go in that direction. He turned right to follow the river. He was happy to be by himself, alone, free, without a care in the world. By chance he found a bookstall still open at that late hour and saw a few books in English. He stopped to peruse and pounced on *The Colossus of Maroussi*. He had a companion for dinner. He had promised himself to read Henry Miller, and here he had accidentally come upon one of his books.

When Marty reached the *Quai Anatole France*, he turned onto the *rue de l'Université* to find the restaurant Sonia had introduced them to in the midst of the *Quartier Saint Germain* where so much of Proust's great book takes place. It, however, was far from the expensive, luxurious, and punctiliously serviced establishment his characters liked to patronize. On the menu the specialty of the house was steak and fries, the common ordinary standard dish of a neighborhood restaurant. The room probably sat at most a couple of dozen diners. The food was good and the service friendly: it was typical of what he thought of as French. He was not inhibited to read his book. Miller starts by referring to the acquaintance who enticed him to visit Greece through her gift of describing her adventures as if using paint. Marty thought it was a gift to be emulated. Miller next refers to letters from Lawrence Durrell inviting him to visit Corfu that blend in poetic language the dream and the reality of Greece, the historical and the mythological, something he found hard to believe until he learned they were true. Marty was persuaded, almost, that reading the book would be as satisfying as a visit to Greece. He indulged in the dream and on the way relaxed sufficiently to comprehend Sonia could be a friend, a loyal friend, both to him and Alex. He concentrated on the book. After he paid the check and started out the door he knew he had nothing to worry about. For the first time in a long while he felt secure in his love for Alex.

Although it was a fair distance, having just traversed it, he automatically walked all the way back to the *rue de Sevigné,* and his comfortable bed.

Marty dozed off clutching his book with the reading light on. He was awakened by shushed goodnights in the hall. Before he had a chance to ask about the opera, Alex's hand was on his mouth. He tried once again with the same result before Alex disappeared into the bathroom. Marty resumed reading his book. As soon as Alex was ready for bed he sneaked up on Marty, grabbed the book out of his hands and tossed it onto his own bed, turned off the light, stretched out next to him and kissed him, deep and long. Marty felt Alex was hard. In one swift motion Marty was turned on his stomach and, without a break, their two bodies were merged into one. The language, the whole-body language Alex spoke, was the language of love. Marty heard Alex whisper, "Feel better now?" Marty communicated his response wordlessly. Alex said, "Are you happy now? I'm happy when you're happy." Marty again squeezed a response with his whole body, for he was indeed happy. He said all he had to say in economical gestures. Alex had returned their Tristan to them. Marty eventually went off into the sleep of the contented with Alex curled up around him.

The following day at dinner, Sonia was ecstatic. She and Alex jabbered on and on about the opera. The seats were, yes, up high, the sound, yes, was terrific. After they described the elegance of the grand stairway and the sense of power and grace it imparts as one ascends to the main level, what impressed them even more was the Hall of Mirrors. At every intermission, they paraded alongside the elite of Paris. Sonia was proud to have been seen with a handsome man, and Alex took pride in the beautiful woman at his side.

"What about the music, you two?" Marty finally asked.

"What do you want to know?" Sonia said.

"Can the lady sing?"

"Marty," both said as they tried to answer at once.

"For heaven's sake, don't joke," Sonia broke out. "It contains the most sensuous music ever written. I go into a trance when I hear it. It may well be an acquired taste, but like everything good in life, you have to work at it. It was sublime, the music, I mean, last night, the orchestra, the singers. I'm not sure we heard her at her best, but she's still good. It saddens me to think it's a farewell. I enjoyed every bit. It was memorable."

Marty noted Alex was uncertain. "Yes—it's so," he said. Marty observed how he worked to produce innocuous language. "Didn't you think I enjoyed the evening? You weren't asleep when we came home, so you must remember something of what I told you."

Marty sensed Sonia and Alex waited for him to react. He thought it was probably not as long a moment as it might appear before he got himself to say, "Good choice, dear Sonia. I'm glad. Our next opera, the three of us, is about a lady called Joan. I hope it's as good. Did Alex tell you?"

* * * * *

It was a Sunday afternoon in November. Marty, Sonia and Alex were sitting in the dining/living room like carelessly thrown jacks. Marty remembered the scene as if it were a stage setting. He was working at the table on the Tribune crossword puzzle. Sonia, hunched over her chair with her back to the table, was deep in the last volume of the Proust magnum opus. Alex, sitting on a chair balanced on its back legs propped up against the wall, stared into space. The sound of the chair plunking down on the floor broke the silence. Alex stood over Sonia and said, "May I borrow a book?"

"You know where." Sonia did not look up.

Alex disappeared into her room and promptly returned to take up his position against the wall. He opened the book. Without warning, he burst out, "In the sonnets – Shakespeare's, I mean – look what I found. Scott Moncrieff stole the English title from Shakespeare."

"What are you talking about?" Sonia said. She sounded surprised in the don't-bother-me tone of someone whose concentration has been broken.

"Listen," Alex went on ignoring her. "And I quote from Sonnet XXX,

'When to the sessions of sweet silent thought
'I summon up remembrance of things past.'"

Sonia, exasperated, said, "Everyone knows about Shakespeare, including Proust. Moncrieff wrote him about his proposed title in English when he was working on the translation. Besides, are you wasting your time reading Proust in English? Didn't know I had it. Read your sonnets—to yourself."

Alex, accepting the reprimand, took Shakespeare back, fussed and fidgeted and fussed some more until he got his coat and quietly walked out. About an hour later, Sonia looked around expectantly and said, "Where is Alex?"

"Out," Marty said.

"Where out?"

"Just out. Didn't say."

"What do you mean didn't say?"

"Just what I said. Am I my brother's keeper?"

"That's a cliché."

"So what?"

"You shouldn't think in clichés. Bloody lack of imagination."

"Alex does not report to me."

"All right. Forget it."

Marty, too, wondered where Alex had gone. Maybe Alex was bored; maybe he should have been more attentive to his mood and less selfish, wasting time with the puzzle. What the hell, it was too late now to think about what could have been. Marty went back to his puzzle. After what seemed like a long time, Sonia piped up with a suggestion to find out what a madeleine dipped in tea tastes like. She first took Marty's replies as making fun, but he wasn't so inclined. It merely had never occurred to him to wonder about a cake dipped in anything. He accepted it as being an odd custom of characters in a novel. He assumed it was a cake like any other. But he suddenly had a change of heart.

"Perfect timing. I've just finished my puzzle. Sure, let's go." Marty liked the idea of what he conceived as a visit to a historical Paris. He had been reading the book, all thirteen volumes, as the full novel finally appeared in 1927, in French, inspired by Sonia, in an attempt to understand what concerned her.

"I feel stupid," Marty said after they stepped out of the courtyard onto the street. "I mean it," he said when Sonia looked at him in disbelief. "You never mentioned that *Madame de Sevigné* has a role in Proust," he went on to explain. "Isn't the narrator's grandmother always reading her letters? Did you pick the apartment on the *rue de Sevigné* because of your work? Or is it a happy coincidence? I hadn't connected the two until you came up with the idea of our tea party."

"Oh my, are you ever the sleuth. Before this moment, it never occurred to me either. One is the street I live on. The other, well, is what I spend my time on. Although mind you, when I am in the *Quartier Saint Germain*, that's another story. I don't think, architecturally, it has changed much. I imagine the characters in their beautiful finery walking past each other as they go about their business. It's a way of life as far removed from us as the Wild West. We can read the letters together, if you want."

They took the side streets in the general direction of the *Avenue de l'Opéra* until they came upon a pastry shop. Marty stopped to inspect the window display and said,

"Look at those Napoleons and raspberry tarts in all their glory. Shall we go in?" He wondered if this establishment would pass muster for members of the late nineteenth century bourgeoisie. He would rely on Sonia's instincts for an answer. He sensed approbation when she preceded him to the entrance and waited for him before going in.

"*Bonjourméssieursdames,*" welcomed them. It was the most complete amalgamation of the three words of the customary greeting that Marty had ever heard. His face glowed with pleasure, which he hoped would be taken as satisfaction in the place they found themselves in and not because of the musical quality of the language. They asked for a table by the window so they could watch if by some coincidence Alex would pass by. Sonia ordered. The owner, heavyset, looked askance and questioned the request. Marty was prepared for her short, dark, wavy hair to curl up in distaste. There were further exchanges. Sonia worked hard to explain that she wasn't disdainful of the beautiful pastries in ordering such pedestrian fare. It was merely that she was doing research; she only wanted to know what that particular combination tasted like. Marty hoped she had convinced Madame that Americans are neither silly nor ignorant, but he wasn't sure.

"I'm impressed by how beautifully you handle the language," Marty said. "But let's get back to research. Am I right that what we are going to savor is supposed to incite memory? From that we may be led to conclude that our natures are outside time—or something to that effect? But my, oh my, it is a long read. Correction: I assume that what we are concerned with is the experience of the narrator, not ours. Is this so?"

"Thanks for the compliment. Stay in Paris a while longer and your language ability will be fine-tuned. You are just too shy to speak unless forced. I have a sneaking suspicion you do very well alone."

"Don't be silly. Tell me about the tea and the cake."

The waitress placed a plate before them with the shell-shaped cakes and a pot of tea. Sonia did the honors. She gingerly placed a cake on her plate. She picked up her cup and raised it lady-like with her pinky in the air to sniff the brew. She similarly raised and tested the aroma of the cake.

"The cake is supposed to have a light citrus favor," Sonia said. "I smell more vanilla than citrus. I wonder if that's right."

"I wonder if Madame sent out to the nearest grocery store," Marty said.

Marty observed Sonia as she picked up a morsel of cake to examine before letting it slide into her cup. She seemed to be inspecting the crumbs as they softened in the liquid to assess the appropriate moment to scoop them up with her spoon. How long to let them soak seemed to be the determining factor. After due appraisal, in one motion she gathered the cake in its liquid and swooped the spoon up to her mouth. She swallowed its contents. She exhibited no reaction.

"I suspect this is a learned activity," Sonia said. She was pensive. "It requires a delicate touch." The second bite she took was of dry cake. "Interesting. I checked the text before we left because I suddenly couldn't remember where the type of tea is described. Is it when his mother serves him the tea and cake that summons the corresponding sensation or is it when his Aunt Leonie offers him that spoonful of tea with the soaked cake? Of course, it is during the *Combray* incident with his Aunt Leonie. It reads, *'infusion de thé ou de tilleul.'* It says one or the other, either an infusion of tea or of the leaf of the linden tree. I guess both can be called tea in English. We generally don't use the word 'infusion' much, do we? We don't drink herbals either. Let's ask for the *tilleul* and see what it tastes like. We'll see—smell—the difference."

Sonia ordered the linden tea. When it came, she removed the top, raised the teapot up to her nose and deeply inhaled the delicate perfume. She put the pot down, paused, reflected and then circled the almost imperceptible cloud of vapor as it rose into her face. "Ah," she said. "It has an enticing fragrance. It's like very delicate lime, isn't it? Infusions must be an acquired taste."

Sonia poured a smidgen into the two cups. Marty raised his and said, "To you." He took a sip, rolled the liquid in his mouth, swallowed slowly and added, "I like it."

"You're being polite. Now that I know what it's like, I've had enough of tea," Sonia countered. "I'm a coffee drinker myself." She seemed to remove herself mentally.

"A penny for your thoughts," Marty said.

Sonia chuckled. "It's probably worth less than a penny. But here is what I was thinking. As you probably know, Proust spins endless stories about his narrator's childhood in *Combray*, the fictional name for *Illiers*, outside Paris, where he spent summers with his family, after he reminisces about the madeleine. This incident and a similar series at the end frames the book. Because the madeleine incident is easily replicated it has become a cliché. But the other memory triggers described towards the end in the last book, tripping over cobblestones and rubbing one's mouth with a stiffly starched napkin, haven't caught the public fancy." Sonia paused. "I have to start reading Henri Bergson, who wrote about memory, and see what Proust absorbed from him. There was much going on at that time about time and space, which forces us also to some understanding of Einstein. I heard that Samuel Beckett, an Irish writer of whom I have just heard, wrote an analysis of the book, which he simply calls "Proust." Much to digest, much to understand. At the moment, I'm trying to conceive of the process, sort of playing games, to aid my understanding, nothing more. Am I rambling?"

"No, but may I ask what you expected to discover from our tea party?"

"I'm not sure. Actually, all I wanted was an excuse to go for a walk and relax. I hope you don't mind."

"Maybe our memory will be triggered in twenty years or so to recall the teashop where we first tasted a madeleine."

"Maybe, but doubtful. Involuntary memory and voluntary memory are not the same. If by a strange coincidence, one of us—both of us?—is in some sort of accident, is severely injured and ends up with amnesia then it may be possible. After a period of years, we return to our normal selves, with no recollection of the past. In due course, we unexpectedly find placed in front of us a raspberry tart—the trigger—and its aroma recalls the tart we had during our visit to the teashop after we first experimented with a madeleine dipped in tea—not very satisfying. Eureka! Out of the blue, we have a vision of our present experience. Epiphany! Very unlikely.

Come to think of it—my example won't quite do. You aren't supposed to be aware you don't remember which would be the case of an amnesiac. What I am trying to explain, perhaps not very clearly, is that involuntary memory is recall of a complete event in the past by a similar event—or sensation—in the present of which there is no memory. Maybe one of us will be blessed—I don't know, maybe cursed is a better word—with the requisite oblivion. I wouldn't count on it."

"How about we go ahead and order two raspberry tarts, if we have finished our research, to complete the scenario for a possible future epiphany. I can't resist," Marty said.

"Yes," Sonia replied. "I'd like that. You realize, of course, neither you nor I are going to be hungry for dinner. Alex will undoubtedly want something. Incidentally, Alex and the Shakespeare sonnet. The way his mind works is fascinating. He has a knack of picking up incredible bits of knowledge with his curious mind, doesn't he? How often do you think one can pick up sonnets and land on the one most relevant? Amazing."

"Yes. He is the prototypical master of incidental information, generally useless, because it interests him. Did you notice how he got hold of the bone on symmetry and wouldn't let go? I can see him at home researching it when we return, assuming he has the time once he starts work. But I bet he manages to make the time. Interesting character."

Marty took it upon himself to do the ordering. Madame approvingly placed the two tarts and the coffee before them herself. Marty thought, if he were in her place, he would certainly grumble about those who come in to eat out of a book. Sonia asked her to wrap up the remaining madeleines to take home. She intimated to the proprietress that she planned to finish them for breakfast. Marty was pleased, for he had neither dipped nor tasted before and would now be able to repair whatever damage he had unwittingly made to his understanding of the meaning of the little cake.

After Marty paid the bill, Sonia wanted to look for the madeleine pan with the scallop shapes. She thought it would be fun to bake her own back in the States. Marty politely expressed no opinion. Madame directed them to a housewares store, albeit curtly, which they found around the corner. When they returned home, Alex was waiting. The light was on in the hallway, but he was sitting in the dark living/dining room drinking wine.

"What's in your hand?" Alex asked. "The package is too big to be a book and too square to be food unless you brought a cake. Where is the string bag with groceries? Are we going to celebrate by eating cake? Celebrate what?"

"No." Sonia said, "No celebration. Sorry. We stopped at a shop where I bought my very own madeleine pan. At some future date, in a city to be determined, when I have acquired the required ingredients and have a fully equipped kitchen with an oven in a proper apartment, I propose to bake the cakes—with your help if you are available and willing."

"So, I'll be hungry for a while longer than I planned. Long time to wait. Just be sure you get a trunk big enough to take all the books and the kitchen gadgets you have collected back with you."

"And where have you been?" Marty asked Alex.

"At the movies."

"You, who rarely go the movies, you went to a movie? I can't believe it," Marty said.

"Yes, you'll believe when I tell you. I was bored watching you two, so I looked in the Trib and discovered a Chaplin Festival. I saw *Monsieur Verdoux*. We missed it, remember, because at home it disappeared suddenly a few years ago, no official explanation given. It turns out it's the funniest movie I've seen in a long time. It's Chaplin at his best."

"Tell us about it," Marty said, egging him on.

"If you want to know, you'll have to go see it yourselves. And where have you been besides buying baking pans? Why no food?"

Marty turned the light on so he could look at Alex. A cantankerous Alex was a rarity. He was the one who had left, and here he was complaining. Marty examined his face and decided he was indeed peeved. What surprised him was that the comment was addressed to Sonia as much as to him. Was Alex envious? What could have upset him so? He thought of the Chaplin movie. A vague recollection tweaked his brain. It was something about it having been withdrawn because it was presumed pacifist, anti-war, anti-American. Here it was, and lucky Alex was the one to have had a chance to see it. Sonia motioned to Marty, pointing with her head to the door. "Let's go," she said.

Marty grabbed the newspaper from the table where he had left it, checked the movie page and said, "If we hurry, we'll make the next show. We have half an hour."

They ran to the *Métro*, onto the train, and managed to catch the movie just in time to get to their seats before it began. On the way home, they stopped for some onion soup at one of the restaurants open late at night around the *Les Halles* market. Alex was not a subject for discussion, although his mood made him an invisible companion.

In the apartment they found Alex sitting in the same dim light, in the same position, in the same place where they had left him, except, Marty realized, drinking a different glass of wine. It was a red instead of a white. Alex, no longer morose, was rather cheerful as he welcomed them home as if he were the host and they invited guests. He offered them some wine, maybe one glass each of the half-bottle remaining. He smiled benignly. After they took the proffered drink, he began to talk about the movie, remarking particularly about what he considered to be the funniest scene, the one in the rowboat. Sonia agreed. In her opinion, the woman's expression, the actress Martha Raye's, when the Chaplin character tries to throw her overboard is worth the whole picture. She felt sorry for the poor Bluebeard wannabe who wouldn't be able to collect insurance as he had for that of his proceeding thirteen wives because he couldn't maneuver her out of the boat and see her drown. Sonia wondered if she would ever be able to think of murder as equating a means to ensure a satisfactory financial return without seeing the two of them seesawing on the boat.

Marty found no sense in pursuing the subject, but felt he had to add a word to show he was participating in the conversation. He commented about it being a work of genius and concentrated on what he wanted more than anything else, which was to change the subject and make peace. It would be easy with Alex in a talkative mood. Whether or not it was the influence of the wine, he would soon discover. He cleared his throat and took his time before asking, "What did you do for supper? I'm sorry we left you so suddenly, but I trust you understand why."

"Oh, but it was my fault. I enticed you into going." Alex accepting the blame was a surprise to Marty. And yet and yet. He couldn't decide. Could Alex, perhaps, have imagined him in a burgeoning relationship with Sonia? Was it because they had spent the day together? Stop it, Marty. Just because you detect Sonia's attraction to Alex doesn't mean Alex is seeing you in a similar role. Maybe it is you who is being paranoid: Sonia is just friends, to you and to Alex, nothing more, nothing less. Better leave it alone, he concluded while half listening to Alex as he went on with, "Now what did I do? I wasn't particularly eager to go down again, so I drank some more wine. I opened the Cabernet we are now finishing. Isn't it good? Eventually I got hungry, so I took myself to the *Place de la Bastille* and found an Alsatian *brasserie*. I had beef and cabbage and sausage and all the good things they pile on a platter. I washed it down with a good beer. Delicious. Then I came back. Here I am ready to share in all you managed to do."

"We went for onion soup," Sonia said. "You know, straight out the door, up the street and to the left. How about we all go tomorrow night when I expect to be back late. Will you hold out and wait for me? Their soup is so good; you must try it, Alex dear. We have to go late, late enough to be early morning to join the regular customers in their fun."

"What a question. Of course we will, won't we, Marty?"

* * * * *

November was coming to an end, and soon after the solstice winter was sure to follow. It was not only the season for onion soup, but time for Marty to show off how to clean and light the coal stove, which more often than not died when Alex and Sonia forgot to feed the briquettes essential to its survival. Marty did not relish the job, and yet invariably discovered he was the only one available when the monster cried out. Alex escaped by becoming invisible when he sensed the coals were turning to ash, while Sonia ignored it by always managing to be elsewhere. Marty hated it because he had to half undress in an ice-cold apartment, when even in better times it was not particularly warm, in order to get his hands fully engaged in its innermost innards. It was time to go home. But, as he learned, Sonia had a proposition Alex could not resist that would extend their stay and further erode their funds. It came as a question when Sonia, the innocent, said, "Alex, I know you like to ski. Want to go for a short visit to the Austrian Alps before you depart?"

"Yes, I do like to ski. How?"

"I've been told of a student trip, very cheap, over Christmas. How about it?"

"Interesting. But Marty and I were thinking, maybe we should be going home."

"Will another few weeks matter that much?" Sonia said.

"Marty, what do you think?"

Marty had ceased to expend brainpower uselessly. Although he was not an avid skier, he had always heretofore willingly accompanied Alex. In any case, Sonia had not asked him. The main question was money, but he and Alex had never discussed their finances with her so she could have no way of knowing where they stood. He assumed Alex was to pay for himself—this wasn't an opera ticket, although, it was amusing to think some tickets could be as expensive as a student trip. What she had paid for Tristan remained a mystery. The adage that two are cheaper than one might be relevant in this case. Would she have in mind the possibility of their sharing a room? Would she be so brazen, would she? Marty refused to contemplate such a scenario. He decided not to venture to guess what accommodations were arranged for student trips. Because group travel was implied, would it work toward participants pairing off? He stopped himself from trying to figure out the possible what-ifs. But if Alex wanted to go, he would not stand in his way. Let him figure out where the money would come from, by borrowing or even miracle of miracles from what remained in the kitty.

"You're the accountant, you should know if you have the money," Marty answered after a long pause. "You're committed to a job. You know the liberties you can take. It's your decision."

What else could Marty have said? What he should have voiced, perhaps, was his unease that Alex and he had already spent more time than was wise pretending they were members of a leisure class whose main occupation is of no more import than surveying the number of squares in Paris to satisfy their curiosity. Sonia had a routine; she had a purpose in life; she was entitled to a respite. Alex and he could offer no justification for an even more extended stay.

"Why don't we go home right after our return," Alex said. "Holiday season is usually dead season. I'll go see the folks at the shop after New Year's and, cross my fingers, all will be well."

Sonia gave Marty a one-sheet note from which he learned that the trip was organized by a French friend of Sonia's who worked in a travel agency. Its purpose was to build post-war a bridge between German and French youth. The woman arranged travel for German students to France and her German colleague did the same opposite for French students. This trip was somewhat different inasmuch as it was to Austria. Probably much the same idea Marty concluded for Austria had been more Nazi than Germany. The destination of the ski group was *Sibratsgfäll* in Western Austria's *Vorarlberg*. The nearest big city was *Bregenz*. Travel was by overnight train on third-class coach. Marty was intrigued and figured if he wanted to go he could say so. He contemplated the possibility for a moment and decided against it.

"We are abandoning you, Marty," Sonia said. "What will you do without us?"

"Not to worry. I may not even miss you," Marty said. "I may want to dream. I will look up every book publisher I can think of, put on my most handsome smile, a shirt and tie, and try to talk myself into seeing the marketing people. If and when I get my own bookshop, I will want to sell French books; and, if I will have made contact—even including a good-looking blond—it will be so much easier later. Won't that be fun?"

"Advance planning is what I admire," Alex said.

"In that connection, how about us getting tickets so we can return to the USA as soon you return?" Marty said addressing Alex before turning to Sonia. "Where will you get the clothing, skis and other paraphernalia you and Alex will need to ski?"

"Our business, not yours," Sonia said. She curtsied to imply she was joking. "My friend will guide us, don't you worry."

Marty was caught in the steady stare of Alex before he heard him say, "We book on the *Ile de France*, if that's O.K. with you. We sail on the 30th. I checked the schedule."

Before Marty assimilated the passage of the activity-filled days, Alex and Sonia were gone. He immediately started on his round of book publishers. Because he liked the area, he tried to weave in a walk along the Left Bank quay facing *Nôtre Dame* cathedral even if it involved a detour. One day as he passed by he couldn't help but admire what he figured had to be an artist's studio overlooking the river staring straight at the cathedral. He had no idea who could afford such an atelier. He pictured an easel poised so the artist could catch the best light coming through the expanse of windows wrapped around both sides of the corner building. He told himself he had to be wearing a beret and a long black cape. He saw him holding the pallet in his left hand and eyeing the nude model stretched out on a chaise longue as he converted reality into an audacious painting of an odalisque. Marty was not sure he was not imagining Manet painting his Olympia less than a century ago. In due course, his dream was shattered when he discovered that that particular set of windows housed one of the city's half dozen or so luxury restaurants. Without a thought, and certainly no consideration of cost, he decided this was where he wanted to be on his last night in Paris. If Alex had found the money for a ski trip, cheap though it purportedly was, he could indulge him with an expensive meal. He made a reservation for three for the 29th of December.

* * * * *

The trio thus came to sit at a table in what was Marty's favorite artist's studio, the *Tour d'Argent,* not as close to a window as he would have liked yet close enough to admire *Notre Dame.* They ordered the specialty of the house, pressed duck.

"Something is up, you guys, when not only do I get the full treatment, but Champagne. What's going on?" Sonia said.

"We're celebrating," Alex said.

"We want to thank our charming roommate," Marty said. "We celebrate having lived like Parisians because of her generosity in letting us share her apartment." He took a breath and continued, "A change of subject, if I may. I haven't heard a word about the ski adventure."

"It was a good trip, don't you think, Alex?" Sonia said. She looked embarrassed.

"I guess we better explain," Alex said.

"The train trip was fun," Sonia said. "We sang, shared food, and, of course, wine. Not much sleep on an overnight ride. In the morning, very early, we came upon a chalet surrounded by snow-covered hills, trees sprouting decorously on the horizon, no sign of civilization. Late afternoon you can picture us drinking hot wine on the terrace overlooking this magnificent view. The food was peasant, Austrian food. I loved the soups. It was good. We got three enormous meals a day, but we certainly worked them off."

Marty was stunned how primitive the facilities were as he heard Sonia describe how they spent their days. He wanted to laugh. In the early morning, they made their way up the mountain by pointing the skis across the hill and laboriously sidestepping up one hill and then another. It was a continuous uphill ski followed by downhill ski, interrupted by periodic gasps for breath or massaging of thigh muscles when they cramped. They schussed down in time for lunch.

"You mean it? You went to a ski resort with no lifts? None?" Marty said.

"True, it's still very Adam and Eve. Before the Fall," Sonia said. "It's a paradise, a wintry Garden of Eden. Very peaceful. Very relaxing."

"It's true," Alex said. "In the afternoon we would ski into *Sibratsgfäll* and have coffee or hot wine. The peasants addressed everyone like old friends; 's'*gruss Gott*' was the greeting. Greetings to God. Charming."

"How about accommodations? Running hot and cold water?" Marty said. He wondered what Sonia meant to imply by referring to the Fall. He was most likely not alone in recalling the consequence of Eve tempting Adam with the apple; Sonia couldn't be implying that in their Garden of Eden she had no apples to tempt Alex, therefore "Before the Fall" means before sex. Bad train of thought, Marty my dear, cut it out, he told himself. Furthermore, you better listen.

Sonia was explaining. "The French have their ways. I paid no attention when we assembled on arrival to the names the leader read off except my own when he assigned sleeping accommodations. Lo and behold Alex and I found we were sharing one big room with half the group. It was like a barracks with a row of beds on either side. We were placed in two such rooms, each holding about twenty beds."

"So, where did you sleep?" Marty couldn't resist butting in.

Alex looked sheepish. Marty was not inclined to read tea leaves to figure out what he meant to communicate, so he repeated, "In the end, where did you find beds?"

"The French kids ran and took what they considered the best ones," Sonia said. "We were all one sex or no sex or sex did not matter. I was glad I had taken my woolly flannel pajamas—they warmed me and covered me well enough for me not to miss a bathrobe. Alex and I finally ended up with adjoining cots. It was quite an experience." Sonia paused, as if asking for permission before turning to Alex, "Shall we tell him?"

Marty, not knowing what to expect, interrupted. He said, "If you want to hold anything back, I don't mind." He intended it as a sort of rebuke to Alex but doubted it made its mark because he phrased it awkwardly.

"Tut, tut, tut," Alex said. "We both love you too much to fool you. Sonia was referring to our adjoining beds which were so close we could hold hands lying down."

"Yes," she said tongue in cheek. "The only problem was that it was cold and the blankets too narrow to extend far enough to cover our hands when we reached out. It was more a mental than a physical exercise. Alex, of course, slept in his flea-market night clothes, which you know well, and added his jacket when he felt cold."

To Marty, it was a cute joke. He could just see them trying to make contact. Could one think of fingers entwined as representing bodies united? Silly thoughts. What could Sonia have been thinking? He decided to change the subject. "What did you do for Christmas?"

"That's when we truly missed you," Sonia said. "It was a clear night with no reflection of city lights anywhere. Alex and I skied to the church in *Sibratsgfäll* for the Christmas Eve service. So simple, so lovely, the little church, so charming. On our return to the chalet, the chandelier in the sky with its multitude of sparkling stars under a full moon was designed to light our way home. It was breathtaking. It's the sort of thing you would have loved. It is so fairy tale I'm not even sure I can communicate the sensation it provoked. We were all alone, not another soul in sight, on the breathless white landscape. Unforgettable."

Sonia looked serene and reposed, her features in perfect symmetry, her skin clear and translucent as she remembered the scene. Marty recalled a painting of a Madonna, perhaps a Memling. Alex reflected her peacefulness.

"And you, Martin my friend, what did you do, all by yourself?" Sonia said.

"You take much for granted, assuming I was by myself. I went to midnight mass." Marty could not decide quickly enough which neighborhood church to name so he decided not to embroider. "I went to *Saint Sulpice*. I wanted to hear the organ. I understand it's one of the best. Albert Schweitzer, who should know, said so. It's true. Come to think of it I didn't even miss you."

"Liar," Alex and Sonia shouted in unison.

Marty took it in good faith they meant it. He, however, wished Alex meant it more than Sonia. He said, "I prevaricate a little. How about a toast to friendship?"

Marty had an odd feeling that for Sonia this could be something like the last meal of the condemned. In a way it was true for it was their last dinner together, at least for the present. "You will soon finish your year here," Marty said. "Soon you will get your degree and eventually a job. We hope at some point you will be able to join us in New York. Then we hope to reciprocate your kindness and share a meal once again."

They ordered another bottle of Champagne and savored the moment enough to feel serene and happy. Marty noted that Sonia was concentrated on Alex. He saw again that expression of happiness on her face he had first noticed when she spotted Alex among the crowd on the terrace at the *Deux Magots* when they first arrived. It was as if she were anticipating the joy of being with Alex again in New York. Alex, tall in his chair, the wild blond curl on his forehead like a swashbuckling hero's, congenial, obviously liking to be liked, charming, and yet, he thought, somewhat detached. Maybe he was imagining it, but to Sonia he must seem real.

"I will be in New York, at least for a while. My dissertation is for Columbia. What happens afterwards depends on where I can get a position," Sonia said. "Let's toast to New York."

* * * * *

Addio a due, adieu à deux, farewell to both was the refrain running through Marty's head in the languages

71

with which he was familiar, as he and Alex huddled in the midst of a crowd on the prow of the *Ile de France* steaming out of *Le Havre*. France was saying good-bye to them. The wind, companion of a ship setting out to sea, dispersed the sound of voices into the void. The speakers raised the level of outcry to compensate, and the din became audible. Alex, his hair blowing in the wind, turned away from Marty to catch the attention of four of the ladies waving handkerchiefs in the direction of the ghosts abandoned on land, eyes tearing, closing a chapter in their young lives. Marty made his way to the rail and turned his face towards the open sea. He couldn't stop the drone in his head of farewell, first in the Italian followed by the French and then finally in English, over and over again, like a melody he couldn't discard. He wasn't certain of everything he had in mind, but he thought one could be his youth that he was leaving behind.

The young ladies surrounding Alex were part of a group returning home after participating in a language course in Paris, or so Marty surmised. They were uniform in appearance, more or less the same height and build and equally well groomed. Instead of the plaid skirts and coordinated cashmere sweaters over bobby socks and saddle shoes, the characteristic uniform of young women in American colleges, they wore plain wool skirts and matching wool jerseys, nylon stockings and European, clunky, rubber-soled, walking shoes. A short visit to France had transformed them into mature women.

Young men, attracted by the beauties surrounding Alex, soon joined the group. The cacophony increased as each shouted to overcome the wind. Marty his gaze fixed on the horizon was oblivious of those around him. He wanted to imprint in memory the receding shore of a country where he had been happy. He was on his way home, as reason insisted, although his heart persisted in raising objections. He wanted desperately to recapture the mood, the sense of contentment, the feeling that all is well with the world. Why did it never occur to him to look for work and so prolong the idyll? Never mind practical details. Unpleasant interludes he overlooked. He wanted to recapture a past he knew could not be retrieved. He ignored Alex. The incessant chatter punctuated by the squealing of high-pitched voices irritated him. He turned towards the staircase that led to third class.

The underwater cabin was crammed with a double bunk, a dresser, a closet and a closet-sized bathroom. Two chairs and a little round table encumbered whatever space remained. The air was musty. Marty slinked down into an armchair to watch the waves slosh against the porthole. He eventually heaved himself up to unpack and, having finished, lay down in the bottom bunk to rock gently as the ship propelled forward in rhythm with the sound of motors in the quiet sea. He fell asleep.

"No time to nap." Marty heard Alex say as he awakened. "We have lots to do."

Alex was smiling and full of cheer. "What in this enclosed floating island besides eating and sleeping?" Marty said half awake. "We've got five days ahead of us."

"Lots of things. To start with there's the young ones you saw on deck. I would have thought they'd want to be home for Christmas, but never mind. Maybe they had better things to do in Europe like we did. They are in second class. Funny the French don't enforce barriers between classes, at least on this ship. But lucky us, I was imparted the secret, the open sesame, of the passageway connecting third to second class." Alex laughed good-naturedly. "I think we're going to enjoy this crossing."

"Were the girls at Berlitz? Is that what I overheard?"

"Right."

"Remember Sonia telling us of some American undergraduates on some sort of French study course, maybe a junior year abroad, the drinking, the partying? Something about being out of control?"

"Vaguely." Alex commented as he emptied the suitcase and put away his clothes. "Yes, I think there was something about them getting mixed up with a rough crowd."

"They probably learned more than just how to hold their drinks."

"Is that cynicism I hear? Don't. All learning is useful. They'll probably be much more fun on this crossing than they were going over. I look forward to investigating." Alex gave Marty a fatherly kiss on the head.

"When do you want to go over?"

"I signed us up for the nine o'clock dinner sitting. We'll go after. Now I'm going to shower."

Dinner didn't lift Marty's spirits. He was overwhelmed by the smell of the wine sauce on his steak, the Brie he loved, the carafe of ordinary wine on the table. He felt as if he were still in a small bistro in Paris. And, in a way, he was. He was dining in an extra-territorial extension of France in the middle of the Atlantic. He was sullen next to cheerful Alex. For coffee, they made their way to second class.

As they entered the salon, Marty could not help but admire what had become of the old tub. When the *Ile de*

France was launched in 1927, her very modern, spacious, neat interiors had been the standard of luxury for the transatlantic liners of the time. In 1939, when war broke out, she found herself in the New York harbor, and the poor lady discovered she had been conscripted by the allied cause. She plied the North Atlantic as an armed merchant ship before she was transferred to the adventurous Far East. At the end of the war, she was returned to the French line and, after two years of refitting, reappeared as a new ship with two stacks instead of three. The simplicity of the second-class salon struck Marty as sheer elegance when he and Alex emerged from her very bowels through the corridors reserved for the crew.

Alex headed straight for the tables of the Berlitz young ladies. The welcome that greeted them conveyed to Marty that Alex was expected. Marty wasn't displeased. It was a cheerful high-ceilinged room with windows facing the sea, and he was happy just to symbolically inhale the salty air. Before he could even make himself comfortable, Alex was on the dance floor. Marty drank his coffee, ordered Cognac and water and sat. The young ladies tolerated him, he sensed, but chose to ignore him. He did not feel like dancing. Alex was prepared to put on the act of the virile heterosexual but Marty was reluctant. He hadn't yet made the transition from France to America.

Good-looking girls attract good-looking boys, and a jolly group ready to celebrate the passing of the night soon surrounded him. Alex was the star of the evening. Marty chose a moment when most of the others were away to whisper to Alex, "Would you say these ladies were the object of the gossip Sonia shared with us?"

"Yes," Alex said.

"How can you tell?"

Alex slunk down to impart a secret. His eyes motioned to the dancers. "See the one in the black dress," he said. "Notice her head on her partner's shoulder. Her body appears to be glued to his. Her partner knows she's no virgin. Remember Sonia's story about the little hotel on the Left Bank where she lived for a month before she moved to the apartment. One night she stayed away..."

"Sure," said Marty. "She went to *Chartres* and when she returned the hotel keeper addressed her as '*Madame*' instead of '*Mademoiselle*' because he assumed what he wanted to assume."

"Well, there is something about how women who are not virgins move. I wonder if it's true of Sonia, though. Never thought about it. Never had occasion to dance with her. She didn't tell us with whom she went to *Chartres*."

"What difference?"

"Just curious. But, in general, different pattern of behavior. I don't think Sonia would ever get involved in the kind of parties these girls did. Not her style. These girls dance with a man in a way no virgin would. Trust me."

"Curious. Where did you pick up all this bullshit on womankind?"

"You dance differently with me now than you did the first time we tried to dance in our rooms, when we first met. Remember?"

"Well. Be careful. I'm watching." Marty laughed. It occurred to him that these young things might be attracted to Alex. And where did Alex acquire all this knowledge about women? From literature? Social intercourse? Physical intercourse? Why hadn't he thought of this earlier? Was it because he let himself be trapped in the black mood that overwhelmed him as the shore of *Le Havre* disappeared? He never imagined Alex attracted to women until Sonia so visibly hungered for him. Could he reciprocate? Did he need to be on his guard from now on? He wished it weren't so.

"Why don't you dance?"

Was Alex asking him to dance? Here? Now? How could he? "I don't really feel like dancing," Marty said. His expression of quizzical wonder seemed to pose the question of how Alex could dare make such a suggestion when he well knew it could cause a riot if they stepped onto the dance floor together.

"Ask the nice one, over there. Name is Nora," Alex said.

"Not now. Maybe later." Marty wondered why Alex was unwilling to understand his lack of desire to dance with anyone, even an expert dancer, although he would not object if Alex wished to practice to prepare for when he would find himself in similar situations after he started at the accounting firm.

"Don't worry. You aren't a wallflower. Nobody cares. Too busy." Alex said. "Order me a Cognac and water, will you? I'll go dance, even if you don't feel like it."

Given that every day the night was shortened by an hour to make up the difference between one side of the Atlantic and the other, Marty and Alex lost track of time. They estimated it was something around three or four in the morning before they attempted to investigate, their addled brain permitting, if the secret door to the passage-way to third class had remained open. They were blessed that one of their new friends, an old hand, was also in third class and knew the way. He led the column of three swaying joy makers to bed as the ship heaved on mountains of water, having encountered the first storm of the crossing.

Alex got in the habit of disappearing early in the morning before Marty was up and reappearing for lunch and dinner. Marty would often see him walking round and round on deck doggedly making his daily miles. Marty devoted himself to reading the two Henry Miller books he had brought along so he could dispose of them before they landed. *The Tropic of Cancer* and *The Tropic of Capricorn* were each considered pornography in the USA, and, if he was caught with them, he was certain they would be impounded. He wasn't sure of the status of *The Colossus of Maroussi* so he left with Sonia the copy he acquired the night Alex and Sonia were at the opera. He was glad he had made an exception to his rule of reading only French while in France because that book enabled him to become acquainted with Corfu from a comfortable distance. The cool fresh air invariably put him to sleep, so the *Tropics* rested beside him, unread.

For New Year's Eve the second-class salon was decorated to resemble an elegant lady willing to dress like a fun-loving creature, not necessarily a streetwalker with pretensions but maybe something similar. It was not in bad taste, although to Marty it was an artificial setting for a scene in which he had no desire to participate. Because it was New Year's Eve, balloons hung over tables and fancy hats, masks, whistles, tooters and other noisemakers were ready to do their part to induce cheer and goodwill. He had an urge to flee. As midnight drew close, he and Alex found themselves alone beside the crowded dance floor. He grasped the moment to whisper, "Alex, please, let's go. I can't stand this artificial atmosphere."

Alex started towards their secret passageway without another word. Marty followed. They stopped at the third-class bar, bought a bottle of Champagne and picked up two flutes. It was with serenity that they approached the coming year as both hands on their watches pointed to midnight. In the quiet of their cabin they raised their glasses in a silent toast, as they looked to life together in new surroundings and an uncertain future with the certitude of youth that they would succeed. They made love and in the ecstasy of being as one they brought the evening to a close.

The next night Marty concluded that the drinking, dancing and gossiping routine was a bore. He had enough and so confirmed that he was a mere observer as Alex realized. Maybe it was his fault. If so, he wasn't inclined to change. He decided to go to bed before midnight but first he ambled over to investigate first class. He enjoyed the view and the décor but found it so stuffy he left after one drink at the bar. He wasn't sure if Alex, who was busy dancing and hardly ever left the dance floor, missed him. It didn't matter. The following night he left even earlier. When Alex returned to their cabin, he was asleep. Alex laid his hand on Marty's bare left shoulder peeking out from under the covers in the lower bunk. He sat down on the edge of the bed, his hand soft and warm against Marty's bare skin. His voice muffled into the pillow, Marty said "What?" He turned around trying to wake up.

"You're angry, aren't you?" Alex said.

Marty raised himself, leaned on his left elbow and lowered his head on his hand. "Give me something to cover up, please. It's chilly in here."

Alex handed him his shirt. Marty wrapped it around himself instead of putting it on. He moved towards the wall to make room for Alex. "I guess so, if you put it that way." Marty wrinkled his nose as if sniffing to discover what was on his mind.

"You fudge," Alex said. "You're angry walking out two nights in a row. What is it? Something I did?"

"Don't think so. I'm not interested. So I get bored. I thought you understood. That's not angry. You figure it out. Too complicated for me. I'm not picking a fight. You know I don't enjoy sitting around by myself when everyone else is busy, when there is nobody left with whom I can talk. I really don't mind your dancing, if that is what you want. I'm happy remembering the way we danced in Paris. That will last me a lifetime. Call it a truce. I'd much rather read my Henry Miller, so I got into bed, started and fell asleep."

"You're hurt. Don't hide it. I know you. I'm the one who hurt you. I'm sorry."

Marty did not respond. His eyes widened in surprise like a cat caught in the headlights of an incoming car whose only concern is escape to safety. He was not sure how to react. Maybe it was the result of the effort to stay awake. In any case, what more could he explain without repeating himself? Maybe he should give it another try. No, not really. In the past Alex was always compassionate and seemed to understand the reasons for Marty's reactions if they differed from his. Did some unfamiliar bug bite him when they boarded in Le Havre? Could it be that the consequent itch forced him to anticipate situations where he would have to compromise and dance only with women so he opted to practice while he had the time? But Alex already had anticipated such situations. Why involve Marty? With pure guesswork, silence may be the best answer.

"Did I abandon you for the girls? Is that it?" Alex went on. "If it is, you ought to know better. Now, please, stop this nonsense."

Marty watched Alex undress and then let him get into bed with him. They lay facing each other.

"Never take what you see seriously. Ever," Alex said. "It's only a game that will last an evening or an afternoon, maybe no more than an hour. I dance. Of course, I do. You don't want to. I know you don't like dancing with girls. But we can't dance together. I would like it as much as you. But it's impossible. So, I dance with girls. It's exercise. It's not lovemaking or flirting or anything like that. All right, maybe a little flirting. It will end when we disembark. I love the ballads, the tangos, the waltzes, and the two-step. I love the sensuousness, the moving in rhythm, the excitement of a step well executed. Maybe I should've been a dancer. When I dance with you, it adds another dimension, a heaven-blessed love that is ours alone. But here we can't. I take second best. You take nothing. O.K. But don't be hurt."

Perhaps Alex was right. Marty examined his brows, his eyes, his nose, his cheeks, his mouth, his chin, each one perfectly crafted and so beautiful and all as much his as his own body. He kissed each one slowly in turn. But Marty couldn't help it. He didn't feel like dancing with girls because it would have erased the memory he cherished of their night in the *Apache boîte*. Maybe later but not yet. Finally, he came out with his "but." "How about the good-looking purser you're always talking to? I know you're flirting with him. I'm talking about the one who brought us cakes to the cabin. Don't tell me you don't find him attractive. I do, but I stay away. How far did you go?"

Marty noticed Alex's face become a mask. It was still beautiful. It was the face he loved but could no longer read.

"What harm can that do? He's charming and wants to feed us pastries from first class. I'm sure he's well aware you and I are a couple. Just a little flirtation. Can't hurt, can it?"

"Alex, Alex, will you never learn that you have charm to spare? Not only with the boys but with the girls. In second class you are the lord. The courtiers and their ladies pay you obeisance. I wouldn't be surprised if the reaction of those select few in the crew is the same."

"I won't argue. Remember though, in the whole world, there is only one that counts, and he is my arms."

Marty noted the mask had lifted as a smile softened Alex's expression. "I'm sorry if I upset you, too," he said. "Tomorrow I promise to dance at least once. I will pretend I am dancing with you. I will celebrate our last night on French soil."

Marty kept his word. The last night on board was a celebration. It was Champagne only. Marty danced with a young lady who was so lithe it was a pleasure. A tango inspired them. They twirled, dipped and kicked. All of a sudden, Marty became aware they were the only ones on the dance floor. Because the music didn't stop, they couldn't either. The eyes of everyone in the room were upon them. When the music did stop, the applause was deafening. They bowed and slowly returned to their tables.

"You didn't dance during the entire crossing," Marty heard Nora say to him. She came around to face him. "You turn out to be the best dancer of us all. Why did you wait so long?" She grabbed him. "The next one you dance with me. Whatever it may be. O.K.?"

Alex smiled. His face was full of love. The next dance was a waltz. Marty danced with Nora and saw Alex go up to another one of the young ladies. After the musicians finally dispersed, good-byes were said, addresses exchanged, promises made, none of which Marty knew would be kept. The ritual, however, was observed.

Marty had no sense of how and when they returned to their cabin. He became obsessed with packing. He felt neither tired nor sleepy. Alex, having gotten ready for bed, climbed up to his bunk. "What do you think you're doing? See the chaos you're creating?"

"I can't see getting up half asleep to put my stuff away before we face the disembarkation procedures, whatever they may be, so I pack now."

Marty threw the two Henry Miller books in the bottom of his suitcase. He had gotten as far as layering underwear and shirts to cover the books when Alex interrupted him. "Are you sure that's what you want to do?"

"What do you mean?"

"Pack in that order?"

Marty continued to pack. "What's wrong with what I'm doing?"

Alex slowly said, "You're going to be unhappy when you have to open that case, if you have to."

Marty, not listening, said, "Don't be silly. I'm almost finished."

When the case snapped shut, Alex stretched out his hand to put out the light and said, "I'll try not to wake you when I get up."

The sun was shining when Marty woke. The cabin was neat. The two suitcases were ready waiting for the addition of last-minute toiletries. At breakfast, Marty was subdued. Alex chattered away. He talked about what he expected on his return after a long absence, about the apartment waiting for him in the Upper West Side, about how he couldn't wait to feel land under his feet. All this talk irritated Marty. He was nervous. He was apprehensive. He couldn't remember what he had done with the Henry Millers. He had meant to leave them with the staff, but he couldn't remember having done so. What had he done? If he had them with him, he was courting trouble. He fretted and wracked his brain, trying to find a trace, a clue to his possible actions. He heard the call for passport control. You're in for it, no choice but to trust to luck, he reprimanded himself as he and Alex saw to their luggage and went to assemble in the lounge.

Marty was startled, after his passport was stamped and he was legally on U.S. soil, to learn his suitcase had been selected for inspection. The pier, although enclosed, was damp and cold. He had nobody to blame but himself and could only hope Henry Miller had taken his books for a walk somewhere on board. He shivered. The suitcase was placed on the ground. Marty opened it as requested. He watched the inspector go through what he thought he had put in neatly but which turned out to be a jumble. He had an urge to apologize but thought better of it. The customs officer poked around, like an automaton, and eventually Marty heard a drawled "O.K." If the officer said anything else, he missed it.

After the officer turned his back, Marty heaved a sigh of relief. He picked up his belongings strewn about like leaves blown in the wind and threw them back into the suitcase. He closed it. Alex meandered over. "Friend or foe?" Marty said.

"Lucky bastard," Alex said. "I tried to stop you last night, but you wouldn't listen."

"I can't remember what I did with the books." Marty said. "I know they're not in the cabin. I went back to look."

"You ass, they're in the bottom of your suitcase."

Marty had an urge to slug Alex but restrained himself. He probably would have behaved in the same way had their roles been reversed. He shouldn't place blame where there is none. "Let's get out of here," Marty said. "Lucky the guy didn't find them. Who knows, maybe they will be valuable someday."

Out on Eleventh Avenue they fought their way to a taxi.

PART II: NEW YORK

Marty ascended the steps of the old brownstone stoop two at a time. With his key he opened the front door and loped up the two flights to the top floor. He paused in front of his door to glance automatically at the one facing it. He and Alex considered the landing their private domain. They kept their doors open when at home. Both doors were closed. Yes, he would make dinner as it was tax season and Alex invariably worked late. He was lucky his bookstore job permitted him to keep regular hours. Marty slowly turned the key, trying to decide if he needed anything from the grocery store and should go down before settling in for the evening. No, he was in good shape. His was a familiar routine after ten years in New York. He and Alex were content with their way of life in Gotham while Sonia was teaching in Chicago.

He entered what in Manhattan is basically an efficiency apartment, an everything-in-one room, a section of one of its walls incorporating the essentials of a kitchen, plus a separate bathroom and a closet. He had created a kitchen area by walling that part of the room off with bookcases. A folding table and four chairs served as a dining area. The sofa bed against the back wall was the centerpiece of the living room, which at night turned it into a bedroom. As he was finishing preparing dinner, music wafted through his open door to let him know Alex was home. The KLH system, tuner, turntable and speakers installed in a ceiling-high cabinet also housing the record collection served as the kitchen divider in that apartment. The system was almost always on when they were home. This evening it was *Così fan tutte*. Marty was glad the Wagner phase was in remission. For the time being he preferred Mozart.

Alex soon crossed the landing. He went directly to the stove, smelled the bubbling stew and gave Marty a hug and a kiss. "Smells like Paris. I'm ravenous. Shall we have a drink?"

Alex opened a bottle of Burgundy while Marty prepared black bread topped with smoked Nova Scotia and sprigs of dill as a snack. He sat down when Alex began pouring the wine. They nodded their heads in a silent toast and drank.

"Silence can be so relaxing," Alex said. "I mean no clatter, only music in the background. What a pleasure at the end of the day to eat quietly. I love you for indulging me. Any dessert?"

After they finished the lamb ragout, Marty cleared the table and put together a scoop of vanilla ice cream and the Crème de cassis Alex liked. He placed the coupe in front of him and smiled. "Yes," he said.

Alex got up to kiss him. "I heard from Sonia this afternoon. Another reason I was late."

"What's the good word from the Midwest?"

"She'll be teaching here this September. She wants to apartment hunt during spring break. I told her she could stay with us."

"Lucky lady; just what she's been wanting. Where do you think we ought to put her up?"

"Silly question. We do what we did in Paris. I'm with you—forever with you. Simple. She'll be in charge of selecting music in my pad."

"When is she arriving?"

"Six weeks Sunday. Thank Heaven, though, when I can spare some time. We better tidy up the mess across the hall. All right, I see you smirking. How about just enough to make room for her to sleep and hang up her coat?"

The days passed by unobtrusively until Alex and Marty betook themselves to Grand Central Station to wait for Sonia to emerge from among the passengers arriving from Chicago. Marty held a bouquet of roses and was convinced she saw the flowers before she saw him. She came directly to give him a hug and kisses on both cheeks. To Alex, she gave a quick kiss before she passed him her small suitcase. In the taxi to the West Side, Marty contemplated the assistant professor sitting between them. She was financially comfortable enough to do what she wanted and he hoped less obsessed with Alex than she had been in Paris. After Sonia unpacked and changed into jeans, they decided to go for a walk in Riverside Park.

As they walked along the Hudson River, Sonia said apropos of nothing, "The sun is beginning to set. Look at that river. It's so beautiful."

"It's the clouds, isn't it," Marty said. He cringed, recalling the evening in Paris when she photographed clouds on the Seine. "You seem to have an affinity for them. What is it?"

"I'm not the only one. Have you seen Constable? Look at Magritte. His clouds are special. They speak to him. They do to me. If I'm depressed, they cheer me up. They are beautiful. They tell me nothing ever stays the same. They symbolize perpetual motion. If the situation I find myself in is not what I would prefer, what I would like, what suits me, I don't worry too much, I know it will change, it will move on, it will become like something other, like the clouds. I would like to preserve these clouds for posterity. Look at the different reds. Lovely."

"Interesting thought," said Alex. "Instead of pursuing it, maybe we better take the time to talk of practical matters. How about the housing situation? I checked with our landlord. No hope here. What do you want to do?"

"Tomorrow I will go to school. I will see what they propose for incoming faculty. I know Manhattan is not easy, but what I need should not be difficult," Sonia said. "Perhaps the good fairy will find me a hovel within easy reach of my classes. Not exactly a hovel, but a place convertible by means of elbow grease into a home."

Marty assumed she was evaluating possibilities. If she had thoughts of an arrangement similar to the one in Paris, he would have to dissuade her. He and Alex were staying as they were. If they moved, it would be to an apartment where they could be together, just the two of them, alone, if ever they would find one they could afford. If one of the apartments in their brownstone eventually became vacant that suited Sonia, he could not possibly object.

Like Sonia's clouds her housing situation was, as expected, fluid. To her surprise, however, it resolved in a matter of days thanks to support from the college. It was exactly what she wanted: a two-bedroom apartment in an older building with easy transportation to the college. She signed a lease starting on the first of August.

Marty, if it had been his holiday, would have spent the remaining few days running from one museum to the other. Sonia had a different idea as he and Alex discovered. On the last day of her week with them, a glorious spring Saturday, they wandered about the city and took in the tourist sites, including Central Park. After dinner in Marty's apartment, in a spirit of celebration, Sonia said, "Alex, before I leave, it occurs to me that I better introduce you to your apartment. I don't think you know it."

Marty and Alex glanced at each other over Sonia's head, puzzled. They crossed over. Sonia pushed the door open, a door uncharacteristically closed all week, even when all three were together on Marty's side of the landing. They entered attractive living quarters, not the storage facility with which Marty and Alex were familiar. Not that it was ever messy, because it was cleaned regularly once a week by their cleaning service. In any case, Alex was by nature neat. The fact is that Marty and Alex lived in what was officially Marty's apartment.

Sonia had scraped and waxed the floor. She had moved the convertible couch so it faced the windows overlooking the Hudson River and placed the coffee table in the middle between two matching salon chairs. She had somewhere acquired a half-moon table that fit between the two windows on which she placed a cut-glass vase filled with fresh flowers. For the side table next to the couch she had found a lamp, which served as a night lamp for the likes of Sonia who liked to read in bed. She had erected a bookcase on the right wall beyond the closet in the middle of which she fitted a small desk. Three Oriental rugs were artfully scattered over the floor.

"Your home," Sonia announced. "Only a dining area is missing. A small table, say for two, or four, or whatever, could be added by the side of the audio system, if you ever want to eat on this side of the landing. I leave that up to you."

Marty and Alex, two statues, without the power of speech, stood on either side of the entryway. "But, but, but," Alex said.

"Yes, baby, I know. A slight case of aphasia, I presume," Sonia said.

Alex shook himself out of his stupor. He took Sonia in his arms and kissed her on both cheeks. "A French thank-you for all your effort, but why did you do it? You didn't have to," Alex said.

"I know I didn't, but I couldn't help it. How can you live like this? I guess men are men. You don't care, do you? You need a woman to arrange your life."

"I'm sorry you went to such expense in time and money. I don't know what else to do except to thank you. I mean from the bottom of my heart."

"Let's go back," Marty said. It came out as an odd stammer. He suddenly had a vision of the young woman in Paris who glowed with love for her handsome escort on their way to Tristan. He shrugged, uncomfortable with the memory and tried to blot it out.

When they entered his apartment, he said, "It's getting late. Tomorrow your train is early, Sonia dear, and we should be thinking of bed. How about a little nightcap, another glass of wine to bid you goodnight and farewell until August?"

Marty was overcome with guilt. Sonia should have understood he and Alex lived together. She therefore, at long last, should have accepted the nature of their relationship, and consequently that neither he nor Alex felt the need to fix what was ostensibly an appendage they used primarily as storage. Wasn't this confirmation enough? She was such a smart lady; she could not have missed recognizing the mess for what it was. She had spent her few vacation days on an endeavor fueled with love, a love for Alex formally unexpressed and unrequited. Surely the evidence before her that it was not to be—yes, but—Marty wasn't convinced. He grappled with the idea of how to put into her head a reality she wasn't prepared to acknowledge. He felt great sympathy for her, for what it must have cost her emotionally, but he couldn't help her.

* * * * *

Spring was coming to an end. Marty wanted help from his parents to secure the basement space he had located off-Broadway, around the corner, on 95th Street. Although small, he foresaw his future bookstore growing out of it. His inquiries had indicated that as his financial situation improved and his business grew, if he wanted to expand, he could eventually go from renter to owner of the brownstone in which it was located. His invited his parents, who had never been to Manhattan, to come for a visit. Within a few weeks they had come and helped secure the rental.

"It's small, but a good beginning. It's a good location," Marty's father said. They were talking over coffee after dinner around the table, Marty's parents, he and Alex.

Alex offered Cognac. Marty's mother was a big woman, black eyes, a full head of gray hair and a contented smile. She said, "It might keep me awake. How about you, Harry? You'll stay awake with me?" It was uncanny the way his son resembled him. He replied good-naturedly, "Why not?" Alex disappeared across the landing.

"You know, the play you suggested," Harry said addressing his son. "The one on Cornelia Street. It was wonderful. What a great idea to provide space, cramped though it is, to give aspiring playwrights a chance to see work performed. I guess you can call it Off-Off-Off - Broadway, but don't quote me. Lanford Wilson is very talented. That's my opinion of this long monologue. The actor portraying the aging transvestite does it so well. Poor Lady Bright, she's so real. So sad at the end of her life."

Marty listened. He was attentive. He was silent. Harry went on. "I was struck that Lady Bright is only in her 40s and is considered an aging queen. I'm older than that, and I don't consider myself old."

"My dear," Lisa said. "We can't stand in judgment of what we don't know. Lady Bright is supposed to be queer. Maybe they feel differently about age than we do."

Marty was pushing down on his chair as if instead of legs it stood on automatic screws that, when pressed, could dig a hole into the floor into which he would vanish. His father seemed to have become obsessed with the subject of homosexuals to the point Marty was sorry he had recommended the play. He had himself not seen it but had gone by the write-up in *The Post*. What his father understood of his relation to Alex, he couldn't guess. He never raised the issue directly with either his father or his mother. As an only child, he basked in their love and affection. He could only be thankful they accepted Alex, whom they treated as another son. So different from Alex's parents who ignored him and, as he liked to say, acted as if they were allergic to him.

Marty unclenched the fists he had clamped on the side of the chair. His mind a rumbling series of discordant musical notes came to a sudden stop when Alex returned with the Cognac. He entered holding a precious bottle of 70-year old Martell. "Get out some glasses, don't just sit there," Alex said. Addressing Harry, he added, "Dad, don't you think the time has come to celebrate?"

Marty set out the big snifters. Alex poured each one-third full. He lifted his glass and said, "To our very own bookstore! And a heartfelt thanks to you two who made it possible."

"Any thoughts on what you want to call it?" Harry said, addressing his son.

"I'm thinking," Marty said. He swirled the Cognac in his glass, sniffed, and took time to enjoy the aroma before taking a sip. He prolonged the act of connoisseur before smacking his lips in appreciation. He knew it was a treat they had been saving for a very special occasion. "I'll tell you in due course. Let it be a surprise."

In late June, Marty went to France. After a week, Sonia, who could never resist an excuse to visit her favorite city, joined him. She had reason. Marty was ordering books and, as a dealer, was entitled to a discount. She wanted a few Proust related and other books and what could be more advantageous than to be with a dealer and share in his bounty. She planned to stay until the end of July.

"I feel like I'm with my lover in my favorite city, wandering from one enticing square to another. Let's take an hour and go visit your favorite *Winged Victory* at the *Louvre*." This was Sonia's litany.

Marty's response invariably was, "My love, after my last appointment, I'll call you. Tell me where you'll be. You can't? Why don't we meet at the *Deux Magots* about 6 o'clock? I'll try not to be late."

Both, without much thought, ended up rambling beyond the *Hotel de Ville* on Marty's last afternoon. As they walked, Marty became uneasy. It was as if he were in a strange neighborhood. Not that he didn't recognize the streets. It was that they were simply foreign. Buildings were shuttered, some appeared condemned, and some looked as if in a state of incipient rehabilitation. The area, they discovered, was to house a national museum of modern art, a public library and a music and industrial design center. It became, as Marty noted, when Sonia sent him a postal card on one of her trips a dozen-or-so years later, an enormous steel superstructure with clear plastic escalator tunnels, brightly colored elevators and utility pipes exposed on the outside. It was formally called the *Centre Georges Pompidou* but it informally was known as the *Beaubourg*. At the approach, a square would take shape on which street entertainers of all sorts would eventually gather to give it the aspect of a perennial fair. Even before it was constructed it already seemed to Marty a foreign country. It was no longer a working-class district. Sonia reminded Marty that the area had once been a beautiful town, hence a "*beau bourg,*" which is what it again would become. They tried to find, without success, the pastry shop where they had researched Proust's first epiphany. They passed right by their former apartment building because they omitted to check the street numbers. Sonia, who spent many a summer in the city, accepted the changes. To Marty the scene was so unsettling he lost any desire to revisit.

That evening Sonia posed the question. "I have no doubt books will be shipped. I know the address. I know your name. And the store's?"

"Haven't decided."

"Publishing houses don't know, yet they agree to send you books?"

"Sure. I pay cash."

"What name have you considered?"

"Don't know. Sometimes I think maybe '*La Librarie,*' but that is so pedestrian, just library, boring. Then I think about '*Libris.*' Plain books. Not exciting. Then I say to myself, O.K. not exciting and not pedestrian, just simple. How about 'Books on 95?' Oh, better drop the 'on.' Plain 'Books 95.' Which do you prefer?"

"How about something vulgar like 'Marty's' or 'Marty's Books?'"

"Yes, I have thought of it, but if the word 'Books' is going to appear, I prefer 'Books on 95' or 'Books 95.' I'll ask Alex. There's time."

Marty returned alone to New York. He planned to open in November. He ordered books, bookcases, showcases, tables, a desk, chairs, telephone service, water service, electric service, stationery, a cash register, toilet paper, paper towels, the long list of requisites, including hiring help. He was lucky that a young colleague named Ben was happy to join him. He loved books and would be an asset. But Marty did not give up his day job yet. He was determined to hold on to the steady paycheck as long as he could. He was comfortable with Alex subsidizing expenses until the store started earning enough for him to draw a salary and again contribute, but he preferred not to abuse this quality of the relationship. Alex took charge of organizing the bookkeeping.

During Labor Day weekend, Sonia completed the move to New York. She invited Alex and Marty to what she called an apartment warming. They came bringing the makings of dinner late Monday afternoon.

"You're here, finally," Sonia said, her way of welcoming them when she opened the door. "I'm starving. Eat first, house tour afterwards, to please the hostess, please."

Marty was shocked when he surveyed the foyer. Bookcases were stacked with books everywhere. It was dark, almost claustrophobic. Then he noticed the pair of doors opening into the living room to the right and the possibility of light streaming in through its windows to break up the gloom. Sonia led them through another door straight ahead through which they entered a long corridor. He assumed the bedrooms and bathrooms led off of it. When they turned into the kitchen, he spied the dining room across the way, connecting to the living room through an archway. He felt better. The apartment faced the East River and light.

In the kitchen the three got busy. Sonia at the counter put together a green salad and transferred the potato salad to a bowl while Alex opened the wine and helped her set the table. Marty carved the deli roast chicken. The flurry of activity ceased when they sat around the kitchen table. The view was over an inner courtyard. It was quiet except for the sound of cutlery. They were hungry. When they finished, Sonia motioned for them to follow. She led them room to room, from the living room to the dining room and ending in the second bedroom, which was her study. The hallway was lined with bookcases as was the study.

"Maybe I should open the bookstore here," Marty said. "I wouldn't have to order books and could save on the rent. Imagine that. I could advertise, 'Used Books – Come Right In.' I could open after you leave for work and close at six in the evening when it again would be your private residence."

"I would scream, 'Stop thief!'" Sonia said. "Help! He's stealing my books. Cut off his hand. Sharia law…"

"Enough joking," cut in Alex. "I need my coffee. Let's have a serious discussion. I need help. Sorry, Marty, I didn't tell you because I didn't want to ruin the weekend."

Again, in the kitchen Sonia brought out cake, cut wedges, and served coffee.

"My parents are coming," Alex said. "They want to come over. I've held out a long time, but no more. They will be here week after next for a few days into Sunday."

Marty had met the parents only once at his and Alex's college graduation. They had made it obvious they didn't like him. It was a visceral reaction. To them the relationship must have appeared like a perversion of friendship. When he was being honest with himself, he realized their disapproval was not based on what they may have judged a difference in social rank but rather a reaction to his person. He doubted they could define the cause for their refusal to accept him, because he suspected it was not rational. What was evident was that they did not apply the same criterion to their son. He could hardly object to a visit but wished to avoid them. Alex was aware of his feelings. He said, "Thanks for keeping the news quiet. We had a great time these few days. I appreciate it. You tried all these years to find excuses, and I guess you've used them up. It had to happen one day. Now it has. And are we ever lucky that Sonia fixed up your apartment. The parents will think you live in a palace."

"I know, Marty. Sorry," Alex said. Marty did not respond. He can't help him. "I should serve them something; maybe drinks and a nibble. Suggestions?" Alex waited for an answer.

What can Sonia be thinking? Marty wondered. What can she make of this talk? Can she guess what the problem is? Does she understand us? If she admits it to herself, she should be able to figure a way to help. I shall oblige and vanish for an evening. Marty trusted his face was inscrutable, but his thoughts, if transformed into speech, could be scrutable.

After what seemed like an eon, Sonia piped up. She said, addressing Marty, "Hey partner, how about you and I do something special for that Saturday night. Say, you cook dinner. We move the table and chairs, the works over to Alex's. I'm the inviting hostess. We serve a sumptuous dinner for four. You disappear for dinner into the Chinese restaurant around the corner and a movie at the Thalia. You return around midnight. We sound the all clear."

Marty's eyes twinkled. He nodded. Sonia had guessed right. Alex glowed. He was in love with both of them. "What shall I say? Dinner at eight?"

Marty shook his head. He was mulling over a menu. "No, make it seven. I don't want to be a night gypsy. If they come at seven, they should be gone by ten."

"Can you make it over by six, Sonia? Or maybe a little earlier? I want to be sure our caterer is gone and you are in charge."

The night of the dinner, Marty returned home a little after eleven. Both doors on the third-floor landing were open to welcome him. The evening was a success. That was Alex's assessment. Marty didn't get the full report until later that week when Sonia stopped by the store to check on progress for the grand opening on the first of November.

"All right. You want it straight; I'll give it to you straight. Dinner went well. They are basically nice folk, not intellectual, but quite intelligent. They may think they are sophisticated, but they are basically small town, limited in their understanding of any way of life other than their own. You know the type. They are what they are. About Alex, they are not open to criticism. He is their beautiful son. They know you live next door. Not hard to guess since they can read your name next to his in the foyer by the buzzers. I wasn't surprised when they asked what you do Saturday nights. We laughed it off implying that each person has his own lifestyle. Alex wasn't prepared to ignore that you and he were friends. Let that pass. I brought a bottle of Champagne and a small tin of caviar. I intended to turn the meal into a festive occasion. You should have seen their faces. Pure delight. To them it became cause for celebration. I'm sorry. It was my mistake."

"Such gesture can't be a mistake. How can it be?" Marty said.

"You're wrong. You'll see. The beef burgundy was superb. The homemade noodles impressed them. Fresh vegetables. On and on I won't go. You know the menu. Alex was a gracious host. The assumption seemed to be that I had been the cook—no intimation that Alex knows his way around the kitchen.

"After the caviar I decided to help only if Alex's hands were insufficient. The parents were getting the wrong idea. They remembered I knew their older son and his family. They took it that Alex and I had been friendly for many years. By the time coffee came they were asking, not even obliquely, what our plans were, fishing to discover when Alex and I intended to marry. From the beginning I felt that they assumed the purpose of the dinner was for Alex to present me for approval. As if to confirm, Mama motioned to look at my rings. I put out my right hand on which, as you know, I usually wear my aquamarine. She grabbed my left hand, which has none. Disappointment was sculpted all over her face."

"It's my fault. I'm sorry to have put you in that position," Marty said. He was panic-stricken, questioning why he had ever let himself agree to Sonia hosting Alex's parents. He felt unable to extend a comforting hand to assuage a hurt he imagined to be beyond consoling. He surveyed the room as if searching for an explanation. He composed himself before continuing, "But come to think of it. It's not mine alone. You have a share because you turned a mess into a charming bachelor apartment. It would never have occurred to me to agree to your suggestion otherwise." Marty was despondent. He tried to puzzle Sonia out. He would have wished to have an inkling of her feelings. He could imagine an Alex concerned about Sonia but emotionally uninvolved. Nothing personal, mind you, it was just his reaction to women. Marty knew him as a caring human being who responded emotionally to young men—to women he responded intellectually. He was convinced he was right. Marty was torn between being jealous and sympathetic. Deep in his being he was sure Sonia still hungered for Alex although she behaved as if she knew it was not to be—at least around him. Still he regretted having put her in such a distressing position. "Was Alex pleased with the evening?" Marty said to change direction. "He said as much afterwards to me. But I wonder if he believes it?"

"Yes, he was a good host. My guess is that, if he needed to change jobs, he could make a great waiter. He was attentive to their every need."

Marty heard but didn't have the courage to ask if Alex was similarly attentive to her. He had to have been. Alex was invariably polite.

Sonia bowed and said, "Before you came home, after cleaning up and returning what belonged to your side, Alex took both my hands in his, hugged me, and thanked me. He was particularly grateful for the Champagne and caviar. He was warm and lovable. He repeated over and over how big a hit I made, how impressed the parents were with my taste and elegance. He laughed and said his mother, he was sure, would be happy to learn our friendship was just that—with my taste I would be an expensive date. His last word was that he was glad it was over."

Marty let it go at that. "Next big event, with a capital "E," is my opening. Will you come and help celebrate by buying a book? Others will be inspired. It will bring me luck."

* * * * *

Over the next weeks Marty plastered the neighborhood with notices advertising the grand opening of Books on 95. Alex was in charge of the wine and Sonia, of the nibbles. Ben presided over the cash register and potential sales while Marty was general major domo. The entrance to the store was down stairs from street level. Marty had set planters with dwarf pine trees on each side of the front door. Inside, facing the entrance, tables showcased recent books, tables with literary journals were placed towards the back while in between, to the extent space permitted, tables were filled with books of every kind conforming to its design as a literary bookshop. At the rear behind a partition a door opened into a room crammed with a desk and a filing cabinet to meet the needs of an office. The walls were stacked mainly with books in English, but a large section in the rear showcased French books. Sonia made sure bouquets of flowers strategically placed made the space appealing and comfortable for browsers.

Promptly at five, people started streaming in. Marty was surprised how many came from the neighborhood and from among their friends and their colleagues. His parents had come to visit again so they could preside as guardian angels. Sonia's mother happened to be in the city so she came to help. It turned into a grand party.

"Congratulations" and "beautiful store" rang cannon-like in Marty's ears. Being that the premises were cramped, the crowd eventually overflowed unto the sidewalk. The old folks, unused to the bustle, opted to leave for a quiet dinner and took Sonia's mother with them. Marty was shocked into awareness of their departure when he missed them and recalled only his father's parting embrace.

The expression on Marty's face became evermore rigid because of the continuous smile with which he greeted the never-ending flow of potential customers until Sonia came up to him and said, "Wipe that smirk off. You need only be charming—not a smiling puppet." She reached up and kissed him right where the laugh lines started, where his face-like mask was most rigid. He relaxed immediately. Embarrassed, he said, addressing those standing closest to him, "I introduce you to my favorite advisor on all things literary, particularly the marvelous tomes behind me produced during the early years of this century in France. That is, of course, if you are interested in French books." Catching himself when he realized what he just said could be ambiguous, he added "They are in French, of course." When Ben rang up a sale, the clang of the register echoed throughout the store as a herald of success. Marty just managed to contain himself. He was pleased with what he had accomplished. Alex, hovering at a distance, was more than surprised at the number of books that were sold on a night usually devoted to making acquaintance. When the last guest finally left, after ten o'clock, Alex, Sonia, Marty, and Ben, although exhausted, sat around the desk and opened the bottle of *Taittinger,* the bottle of Champagne Marty had bought at

"Duty Free" for the occasion when he returned after his last visit to France.

Two weeks later, when Marty was getting ready to close, the phone rang. It was Alex. It was a beautiful fall day with clear skies. Alex had decided to walk home from work, so he said. His story as Marty remembered was that as he was sauntering down Broadway and crossed 39th Street he noticed the crowd milling around in front of the Metropolitan Opera. He was enticed to stop. The rest of the conversation was a series of clipped phrases as Marty would later relate that almost exhausted him. Alex saw a man wave a ticket...cheap, for tonight, Row D, Family Circle...good seat...wife had other ticket...had to go home and take their dog to the vet.... an emergency...a believable story...not a scalper...right price...bought on impulse...just enough money...no time for dinner...afraid quarter running out. Before hanging up Alex said he'd grab a hamburger with just enough time before the performance was to begin. Marty put the receiver slowly in the cradle exhausted by the tone of the conversation. He had no inkling what opera had caused Alex to agree to gobble down a hamburger. Marty couldn't remember the last time either of them had had a hamburger on the run or otherwise. Marty, disappointed, took himself to the Arab restaurant on Broadway. It was the night Alex was to cook. Sitting down and being served is what he deserved.

At midnight Alex came home. He greeted Marty with a grin deserving of the Cheshire cat. "Guess what? You won't believe. This is an incredible city." Alex said.

"You went to the opera," said Marty dryly.

"Yes, later." Alex was excited and disgorged what he had to say without waiting. "During the first intermission, the couple sitting next to me addressed me. I was uncomfortable. Their questions were intrusive; too personal. Afterwards I concluded I was being interviewed. Everyone in those seats knows everyone. It was like an extended family, all married to their seats for years and years. Like family, they knew each other's business and occasionally squabbled like old married couples do. One man knew how and why I had bought the ticket; he knew all about the sick dog. They talked opera. A well-informed discussion covered the field, the operas they liked, favorite singers, lousy conductors, memorable evenings, favorite recordings. It was during the second intermission that the wife informed me that they had an extra subscription they would let me have if I wanted it. I almost passed out. I have been trying to get a subscription ever since we came to New York with success never even a fleeting thought. Here I almost became the proud owner of a subscription for two. We exchanged addresses and arranged to meet before the next opera when I could give them money in exchange for tickets. Here I'll show you the slip with the address. I'm so happy I could yell from the rooftops." He flopped down on Marty and kissed him. "Can I call Sonia and tell her? Will she be furious if I wake her?"

"She's crazier than you about opera. Even if she is initially upset, she'll recover. If you want to, do it. If she screams, pass me the phone."

Alex dialed. On the sixth ring he nodded and said, "Sorry to wake you. Truly sorry ...But you must hear ...I got two subscriptions to the opera for the rest of the season. For you and me. I just got them. Such a fluke. Is it terrible to be awakened for such news?"

Alex smiled, shook his head, pleased. Marty dozed off. He was roused when Alex rattled off that it was *Il Trovatore* with Leontyne Price, Robert Merrill and Richard Tucker. "Unbelievable, the cast." Marty heard him exclaim, "I was in heaven. I wish you could have been there. But you'll be there for the next one." As he was falling asleep, Marty heard through a haze, "Marty? Marty goes to the opera when he has to...our backup...No not left out. Remember our night at the opera when we did go together? But...he bitches...honestly...no room for legs...not yours...he won't go. Maybe someday...better seats...more room maybe...we can convince him...G'night."

"Now I know we are New Yorkers," a half-asleep Marty heard Alex say as he reflected and muttered, "Good night to you, too."

* * * * *

Marty's mailman handed him an envelope one busy late afternoon at his book shop. He had politely summoned Marty to give it to him separately from the office mail, which he customarily dropped on the cashier's desk. He put it into Marty's open hand because he probably intuited it had nothing to do with books. Otherwise why make him walk all the way from the back in view of all his customers and staff? Just for a letter? Nice of him but unnecessary. After years of delivering mail, he probably knew as much about the business as Marty and Ben. If he assumed it was a secret letter about an assignation in a far-off land Marty couldn't wait to read, he was wrong. But why worry? He can think anything he wants. Ben, kindly, scholarly, gentle

Ben, the personification of a knowledgeable bookstore attendant would have passed it unopened. He knew all there was to know.

Marty didn't do business with Peru. So why Peruvian stamps? Who could it be—from Peru? Where? The stamp? Hard to make out. Marty slowly read aloud, "Eye, Cue, You, Eye, Tee, Oh, Ess." Upside down there was another similar. Never heard of it. How to pronounce it? Eyekeytos or Eekeetoes or Eyekeetos? Any one of them he guessed could work. Handwriting familiar. Looked like a Sonia scribble. What was she doing? Wherever there was a there, she was there. He knew she joined Alex in Mexico and afterwards was to go on to her usual summer haunts in France. South America hadn't figured in her conscious universe. Not that Marty knew. Alex came back and left again and came back again. Said little. He was all work those days. Why did she write? Never before had a letter from her. A postal card? Sure. But a letter? The stamps covered half the face of the envelope. Must have found only small denomination stamps. Did she think Marty was a stamp collector?

It felt so thick Marty's callused fingers couldn't estimate the number of pages. Couldn't see through it, couldn't even with the help of the fluorescent light beaming down from the ceiling when he raised it and turned it upside down. Proof of weightiness, in ounces, that was. Didn't smell like anything either. He was hoping it would divulge her presence by its scent. What is that musky perfume she likes to wear? Wait, yes, it is *Le Tabac Blond*. It is by *Charon*, he thought. He'd never know why it was named blond tobacco. Wasn't it supposed to be the best smoking tobacco? Something like that. She always thought it was the best smelling perfume. He remembered buying her some at the *Lafayette* department store in Paris.

Was she writing a book on which she wanted Marty's opinion? First chapter enclosed, please comment. It was sealed and didn't divulge any secrets. Did she expect him to answer with no return address, at any rate none on the envelope? Eventually she'd be back home, and then he could respond, if need be, to whatever she asked, unless, of course, there was something she wanted him to do, in which case, he'd report. Damn the envelope, it had intrigued him so he didn't know how he managed to walk back to his desk—it was a long way from the front to the back—but there he was. Marty pretended he was Sherlock Holmes examining an unexpected piece of evidence. Of what? Who knows? Reluctant to be caught in the act, he furtively reached for the letter opener. It went slts... slts... slts and the envelope was ready to disgorge its contents. Out came the bundle of paper. First page:

Dear Martin, Marty, my dear friend, my favorite Martini,

Good grief, what a salutation! Was it meant to butter him up or flatter him? He looked closely and decided it was Sonia's handwriting. There was a letterhead. A hotel in *Cuzco*. Fancy hotel provided paper. No dateline. Let's see last page. Aha! It was signed Sonia. And with much love. That's what it said. Was she sick? Where did *Iquitos*, if that's what it was, come in? Where was she? He heard himself say, "Let's find out."

Why am I writing to you? There are many possible reasons. Any of them real? Some to be sure. I may simply want to tell a story to someone who I know will understand it as intended. Another that might perhaps not ring false is that I am sitting with a loose pen looking for a pair of considerate eyes to read what it writes. Let's say I want to try out a new story line on you and see if you accept it as gospel truth. I may want to confess my sins, venial I believe, to one I trust more than I do a father confessor or a psychologist or a psychiatrist were I a practicing member of any such faith. The simple truth may be that I crave absolution. I have no one to talk to, so I write. To you.

Ben on the intercom startled Marty. "Pick up" is what he heard. He absent-mindedly lifted the handset to his ear, "Marty here," he said, his eyes on the letter. "Yes, we do have it...I'll be glad to put it aside for you...you can pick up at your convenience." He read, "... crave absolution..." He couldn't make out exactly what the voice on the telephone was saying, so he automatically advised, "Yes, we are open every day except Sunday until 7 p.m...." He must have answered correctly. As he hung up, his thoughts echoed his standard litany about Mr. Stevens who was a good customer but demanded personal attention. Marty wrote out the book order. "Should try to pass this character on to Ben who knows as much about books as I do," Marty muttered.

Where did Marty leave off? Oh yes, she craved absolution. He read again,

> ...The simple truth may be that I crave absolution. I have no one to talk to, so I write. To you.

What on earth could have happened? And who is he to give absolution? He's not going to start that jealousy nonsense, is he? Alex and Sonia were on a trip together. Not a new development. So why should he be concerned? Read. Find out. Be quiet. How stupid to assume that it is he, Marty, who can give absolution to Sonia or to anyone for that matter. What could it be? He read on.

> The story begins in Mexico City. Alex, as you know, went for a meeting. He badly wanted a companion, an escort, a partner. He sent me an SOS to join him. It was full of excuses: he didn't know in advance, he hoped I wouldn't mind the short notice, could I please not go to Europe just yet and join him, please, please. Nothing new. I have been his 'lady pal' for years.

Marty skimmed a page full of description of parties, tourist sites, the clothes each wore to what. The meeting concluded. And pages and pages to go. What is she doing? Nonsense is what she writes. Vernacular English too much for her. Must be drinking. Wonder what she's drinking? Of course, all eyes were probably on her more than on him. Yes, they do make a handsome pair. Marty would flatter himself that when the three of them are together all eyes similarly are on them. Who is the one that draws the bees to the honey? His bet is Sonia. If she could read his mind, she'd probably tell him right now to stop thinking in clichés. Nothing new. Used them before. Probably more than once. So what! On with her letter.

> Now, hold on, and I'll tell you what he aimed for. Are you ready? He wanted to go to Machu Picchu. Since I'm writing from the neighborhood you do not need me to tell you that I agreed to follow. I will go wherever you go sort of thing. The low price on the next departing plane took us to Buenos Aires. Not the most direct route, but it

was much cheaper than a direct flight to Lima so there was no discussion. And Buenos Aires—what a city!

Marty skipped another page or two, as they were working tourists again.

...We spent a few enjoyable days there before going on to La Paz in Bolivia. Crazy but it made weird sense.

"Good for them," Marty muttered. What else did they do together at something like 12,000 feet?

...Alex decided it would be fun to go around Lake Titicaca on our way to Peru. Surprised I was, really, to find just such a tour.

The next few pages, if Marty was not mistaken, indeed read like a travelogue. He didn't understand if he was meant to be inspired to follow in their footsteps. But was he supposed to be interested? She damn well knew he wouldn't leave his books. Why all this description engorged with quotes from brochures and their guidebook? Was she avoiding the reason for writing? Delaying? Nothing about Alex, his reaction, his behavior towards her, what they felt, singly or jointly. Odd. Marty didn't get it; she could wait and tell him instead of wasting paper and postage. Let's see where I'm taken next, he told himself.

We lunched at the Copacabana (remember we are in Peru not on the beaches of Rio) on the other side of the lake and started on the way to Puno.

Marty skipped her story of roads and churches until he caught sight of *Puno*; it forecast a metaphorical change of scene, politically, he guessed, not geographically. He read on.

Every place on the road there were stops. It seems the vehicles are only licensed to operate within limited areas and those going beyond need special permits, which have to be controlled at practically every village. The border consists of a hut with one official; currency control is a separate stop. Late in the evening we came to Puno. It was already dark. Look it up on the map. It's in southern Peru. It's supposed to be beautiful as it is located on the shores of the lake in the midst of glorious mountains. Must be, but we did not have a chance to find out. We arrived in the midst of chaos. We could not get anyone to divulge the reason. In La Paz I had heard that there were problems due to a dispute between professors and the authorities in Puno and Arequipa as a result of which the students had gone on strike. Eventually when we got access to a radio it broadcast nothing informative. Martial music mostly. We discovered that those tourists who were supposed to move on and vacate their hotel rooms couldn't. Hence the room status was none available, nil, nothing, nada, reservation or no reservation; it was useless to argue. The workers on the railroad had gone on sympathy strike, hence no train from Puno to Cuzco on which we had bookings. There were no busses either because the drivers had similarly walked off the job. We were stuck in Puno with nowhere to go and no place to sleep. Why we were allowed to proceed from La Paz is a mystery. Curfew was announced shortly before we arrived. We were dropped at the hotel and were theoretically restricted to a hotel lobby with others in the same stew.

Alex asked me to see what I could do at the desk while he snooped around. I admit we were treated royally, given the circumstances. Somehow, probably with a magic wand, the clerk produced a room, one for both of us with private bath. No questions asked curiously enough in a Catholic country. He must have known we had reserved two single rooms, but how could I reject a whole room to ourselves? At least we had a place to sleep—for the night. I told myself this is no time to worry about Alex's reaction. I reminded myself that once, years ago, we slept in adjoining cots in Austria on our famous student trip. This night we'll again sleep in adjoining beds. We survived then; we'll manage now.

The cliffhanger needed a drink. Yes, Marty remembered the story about arms bridging the gap between beds. He needed reinforcement to get to the end of the *Puno* saga. The store would close soon. Then, with drink in hand, a hefty Scotch—straight—he would follow the adventures of Sonia and Alex. He saw to it that customers completed their business, bid his staff goodnight and waited for Ben, the last to leave, to close the door behind him. Marty returned to his desk. He didn't know when Alex would be home. He didn't want to face him until he understood the reason for the letter. Up went the glass. "Cheers, Marty, to resolution of the *Puno* puzzle," a voice, Marty's, echoed in the now-empty store.

A bubbly Alex came back, eventually. Exploration concluded successfully. He had struck up a conversation with a tour group of Germans with their own bus. Tomorrow they leave for Cuzco. Could their guide somehow squeeze two more bodies onto the bus? And guess what? He could. We had a way out! And who knows if we could keep the room another night.

We were ravenous by then. It was late, so we stepped out to look for a place for a bite. No need to fuss. Eggs with the vegetables available became a Spanish omelet. And a glass of wine—lucky the little restaurant did have wine—not bad—and ending with coffee and a cake for my sweet tooth, turned it into a royal repast. We returned under curfew, but no problem: there were others on the street. The militia ignored us all. We planned to go to our room since we had to get up early as the bus was scheduled to leave promptly at eight.

Until we opened the door, I had not given thought to what we would find. I had given the bellboy a tip to take our bags to the room. They were there, two on the luggage rack and the hand luggage nearby. The room was a double, yes, double, with one double bed. Just one bed; no other bed or couch or anything to sleep in except the floor. I expected two single beds. It never occurred to me to ask. I didn't know whether to look at the ceiling or the floor. I peeked. Alex laughed. I followed. I guess it was silly laughter, but it gave me the opportunity to suggest that since it takes me long to get ready for bed why didn't he go first. We were both exhausted.

You will forgive me, but I couldn't help myself. I had over the years we have known each other hoped, aspired, yearned, wanted to be, how to put it, romantically involved with Alex. Many a time I found myself in a situation that mimicked such a liaison. I don't think I am writing anything, Marty my dear, to shock you, because I have suspected you have always known, known from the very beginning. And here to find myself in the midst of a setting conducive to such an amorous encounter was more than I could ignore. I hadn't chosen it and neither had he. It was not perfect. I could think of many another setting I would have preferred. But we do have to take advantage of opportunities that unexpectedly present themselves, don't we?

I sat on the bed and imagined what it would be like if we made love, tired as we were, before going off to the sleep of the blessed. I was so far off into my own little unreal sex impregnated world that I was unaware that he had come out of the bathroom and climbed in on the other side. What I felt was a sort of weaving up and down on a mattress becoming a raft hovering in the middle of the ocean.

Now Marty knew why the letter. Did he read ahead to get to the meat? No, no, not meat. He didn't want to think flesh. How about the point? That would do. He could hear Sonia telling him again and again to stop thinking in clichés. He couldn't help it. Should he continue to pretend that Sherlock Holmes, without an inkling of what the future held, was waiting to discover the clue that would lead to the action foretold? Or lack of action?

Suddenly, out of nowhere, Marty remembered Charlie Chaplin trying to throw Martha Raye off the rowboat, hopefully to drown. He could see it now: he had gone with Sonia to the movies after Alex told them about *Monsieur Verdoux* when they returned to the apartment after going to a teashop to taste the famous madeleine dipped in tea. A Sonia, rather a Proust, epiphany is what he had just had. With trepidation he wondered what Alex would do with her on their raft.

He decided he'd have another drink. If Alex were home, he'd have called. No call, no Alex. He could stay and drink—and read. There went the Scotch. A good slug. It should squelch any evil thoughts of sex that might opt to intrude. He felt better.

I, like a jumping bean, leaped off in a blast. Translation: He caught me unawares. I turned around and saw only his head looking at me from beneath the bedcovers. I snickered and told him he had surprised me out of my dream world. He apologized and suggested I get to bed as I must be as tired as he. I took my kit into the bathroom. I had to come back out because I had forgotten to take something to change into. That was a problem that on this trip I had skimped on a nightgown in favor of fancy dress. I remembered I had a full slip somewhere in my case and decided it would have to do. It took me a while to find it.

When I finally got into bed, I found Alex on his side, turned towards the opposite wall. I nuzzled up to him to whisper into his ear something like a sleep tight good night, which I hoped would turn into the initiation of— no need to spell it out. He had evidently also omitted to pack pajamas. He was out, out of this world. I mean literally—out. He probably never sensed I had stretched out alongside, my body flat against his. It was like, how shall I put it, like attempting to make love to a corpse, except this one was breathing besides being warm. I had taken too much time in the bathroom, enough for him to have fallen into a sleep so deep he wouldn't waken. At least, that's what I told myself. I couldn't believe any human being could pretend sleep with another pasted up against him. But he did. Sleep, I mean.

Was she kidding? After dinner they must have stopped off to try the local coca. It must have been a secret potion— each one indulging in a different variety. What opera had they heard to inspire them? She wrote there was none in *Buenos Aires*. She didn't mention any in Mexico. It must have been last season at the Met. What could it have been? Could Alex have been pretending he was Juliet and took a sleeping potion like the one Friar Laurence gave her to induce a simulacrum of death? But instead of awakening in expectation of finding his Juliet, Alex decided to sleep until morning. What was Marty thinking? Stop it, he told himself. Maybe he took the wrong potion. Sonia must have assumed she acquired the love potion Bragane gave Tristan and Isolde. Unfortunately, it was another she unknowingly gave to Alex and consequently finds herself lying next to an inanimate body. What if instead they drank too much cheap red wine at dinner, not an elixir such as the supposed Elixir of Love, but a better one? This opera alluded to a version of the Tristan story, didn't it? Alex drank so much he passed out. Sonia handled her liquor better and simply became amorous, exactly the effect anticipated. Not funny. Not at all. She would have been better off sharing a love potion with Alex. He was a good sleeper, but not that good. His skin, all of it, had very good sensors for making love. Marty knew. Alex had said very little since he returned. No details, of sex or anything else, no nothing this time. All right, Marty. Just remember you and Alex are an old married couple. Like all spouses one may sometimes stray. Relax. Some. Not all. Have another Scotch. Remember Alex does...what? Not respond to women? If he were interested in Sonia, something would have occurred before now. Right? Put your bouts of jealousy to rest. Slightly soused? Maybe not; maybe not enough. Back to failed lovemaking. This scenario must end soon. Read on. You try to believe her story because you have to believe.

> ...I didn't think I would be able to fall asleep after my erotic charge, but I guess I was so tired I eventually did. Morning, I had hoped, would offer a scenario in my favor, but I was wrong. I felt a hand on my shoulder and a voice

waking me; it was 6:30, and if I hurried, we would have time for breakfast before the bus came. Alex was showered, fully dressed and perfectly shaved.

Eureka. Saved. Feel better, Marty? Yes, Marty. Here goes, to Scotch!

The Germans were pleasant. The bus ride was not the most comfortable because we were sitting in the back row and bounced all the way to Cuzco. It was nine o'clock by the time we left. The Andean altiplano, needless to repeat, is beautiful. We reached some 14,00 feet at the highest point. We saw wild and domesticated llamas; we stopped at thermal springs. After we reached the highest point the terrain changed ..."

On and on it went.

...By the time we got to Cuzco it was about 6:30. We went to the hotel where we had reservations to discover management was convinced nobody was coming from Puno and cancelled ours. After Alex put on an angry face the clerk found us a room, again a double. This time it had twin beds but faced a shaft next to the kitchen. Dreary and dingy and noisy, but we managed to get some sleep until the refrigeration machine started off promptly at 5:15 in the morning.

The first thing we did was to check into another hotel right off the Plaza de Armas, the central square. Two rooms with private bath, mind you on separate floors, was the unexpected luxury. We arranged for a city tour of the Inca ruins...

Marty stopped reading. Words jumped at him: *Cuzco*, disturbances, riots, army, curfew, lucky train, *Machu Picchu*, *Urubamba*, *Cuzco* again. First Sonia told Marty to go read a guidebook, and then she turned to writing a guidebook. He would venture to guess, my dear Watson, the dear lady is putting off getting to the point. If nothing else, the letter was turning into a record of their trip. Good to read in twenty years to jog memory. Marty, time for you to have another drink. By the thickness of the paper remaining, he estimated he might be getting to the end. One more drink should do it. The nice bottle of Scotch said, "Here, pour yourself a nice drink." "Thank you," he replied. For heaven's sake, don't swallow so hard. That hurts. Go on, get it over with.

> Amazingly at Lima airport, people accosted us asking what happened in Cuzco.

Marty skipped a page.

> Alex, as you surely know, remained at the airport and got a plane home. I went into Lima myself. I contemplated. Not enough time to do anything in France. Why not explore the Amazon since I'm close, relatively speaking. I decided to go to Iquitos and investigate how to float down river, at least as far as Manaus and its opera house. Iquitos, if you want to know, at the headwaters, and Manaus, sort of two-thirds down river, were both made rich by the rubber trade at the turn of the century...

That solves that little mystery, Marty my friend. Maybe the next page will solve the bigger puzzle. Yes, here we are.

> Now to the why of this letter. Remember the scene in Proust when Swann is on the point of kissing Odette for the first time and possessing her? The anticipation he feels is delicious in and of itself. Remember what goes

through his mind as he holds back to give himself time to catch up with his dream? He compares his view of her face to a landscape which the traveler is seeing for the last time, that view which he would wish to retain to take with him on the day of departure because he is leaving the place forever and will never return. I won't quote the French to you except for the last phrase: ...*on voudrait emporter un paysage qu'on va quitter pour toujours.* You can look it up. It is sheer poetry to say one would wish to carry away a view, or landscape if you will, which one is leaving forever.

The mystery that awaits Swann exhilarates him. I saw a sleeping face when I brushed my lips against it; I studied the face; I anticipated the mystery of possession. I anticipated retaining a memory of that face the way it looked at that very moment—may I use the word virginal to describe it?—which I hoped never to see again looking exactly like that. Swann possessed. I may never possess. I use 'may' because the chance of possession—accidental or preconceived, whichever—is difficult to anticipate for all eternity. But I will see that landscape again. I am a returning traveler. I will keep seeing it, perhaps somewhat modified by the effects of time, but otherwise unchanged, unchanged by possession, possession by me.

I can't help thinking of Swann's fumbling with the orchids—*cattleyas* in Proust's terminology—on Odette's bodice as he dawdled to delay the act of possession. To them thereafter the allusion to *faire cattleyas* came to mean to make love. Of course, Alex and I will have no reason to create a private language to allude to an act that never should have been. I have something else instead, something precious I do not want to give up. I call it friendship. Even the word love may apply, but it is a different type of love. That love includes you. I don't want to lose Alex. I want you both, not either one or the other.

I'm afraid that somehow, somewhere you will ask or we will talk about this trip. Along the line, either Alex or

I will come out with something related to this new chapter in the story of beds. They now total three. I can't guarantee there may not be more because there is always another occasion that may arise and become number four. I can't expect you to believe that two can simply sleep, only sleep, next to each other. You did not question the story of our Austrian attempt to clasp hands, only hands, across the divide between two cots, even though unsuccessfully. One explanation could be that we were not alone but two among many. A certain lack of privacy is a consideration.

I suspect you have known since the day we met that I was in denial. I would not admit that you and Alex were a couple. I noted how Alex's parents reacted to you but refused to conclude as logic dictates. Your two-studio setup is a dead giveaway, but I took it as a clever arrangement of living space. The evidence was before me, but I rejected it. What I lost in that bed in Puno is not my virginity, had I had it to lose, but my capacity for denial.

I asked at the beginning if you will believe what I write—assuming I mail it. I'll see. What's truth? It is said that in wine there is truth. How does it go? In vino veritas? I have indeed written most of it in company of a bottle, my favorite local brandy, called Pisco. (P.S. I have a bottle for you. I want to share with you what I like.) Maybe, therefore, it is true. I report on rumor, which may not be trusted, depending on the source. I don't cite sources. Do you believe me? I leave it up to you to decide if you will absolve me of hurting you. What I treasure is your love. My bottle is empty, almost. Here goes to us, to our friendship forever. Yes, to be sure, I'm soused.

Did Marty believe her? Maybe. Yes, but all the same, he didn't. He wanted to believe. He had to believe. And yet why did she, even if inadvertently, plant a doubt. But if he didn't believe, it presaged the end. But it can't end, because of Alex. What about Alex? He trusted. It could be false trust, couldn't it? No. He had to trust, plain trust. He loved Alex and couldn't envision living without him. And yet, he knew but would not openly admit that what Sonia had written was a fable. Like all fables it hid a truth. He had no choice but to go along with the fable, at least for the time being, although it could stretch into forever, depending on what the future would bring.

Yes, he had always known. Yes, Alex is many-sided. Yes, jealousy hides in full view. Sonia wrote a long funeral dirge to put it to rest. She may have succeeded. He was not inclined to give in to jealousy, and instead become accustomed to accepting the inevitable. One last Scotch for the evening.

Whoopee! Was he drunk? Probably. Alex won't like it. A mouthful of parsley will kill the odor. He won't guess, not much, he hoped. No supper yet. Get home, make supper. It's not so late. Alex will show up. Eat. Yes, make love after. He'll never guess why. Get even with *Puno*— what did or didn't happen. To paraphrase Mr. Pepys: And so to home.

A couple of months later Sonia came by the store to pick up a book. It was closing time. She was in no hurry. After the staff left and Ben closed the door behind him, Marty opened a bottle of Sancerre and brought out glasses. They chatted around his desk. Marty looked at her and saw her for the first time what she had become. His vision of her had never wavered from the way he remembered her in Paris. She had been like a rose, a bud, the petals fresh, bound tightly, exuding the aroma of a rose in the first blush of youth, with the promise of the beauty it would divulge when it burst open. Time had interceded and the rose had opened in full bloom. It was beautiful still, but the edge of the petals was crinkling, the first sign of the ravages of time. Marty hadn't noticed as he had ignored it in himself when looking in the mirror every morning while shaving. Yes, he would have to admit they were both beginning to age, the spider busily weaving wrinkles around the eyes and mouth as if enclosing the fading rose in its web.

After one glass of wine, Marty felt he could broach the subject of the letter, to which up to that time neither had alluded. He poured a second glass. As he set the bottle down, he said, "I was wondering, in your ever so long letter, as I read the description of where you went, what you did." He stopped as if to collect his thoughts. "Why you said so little about Alex, how he reacted to the places you visited, so little about how you reacted. As a factual record, yes, that it is. All that description is, however, irrelevant to what you wanted to say."

Sonia giggled. "You said it. I can't explain. Maybe, yes, I can. I knew what I wanted from you, but I didn't know how to ask for it. I guess I couldn't face it. It took time to get there. So, I started at the beginning of the trip and set about to describe—what?—physical actions, the terrain, the irrelevancies. I first wrote in *Cuzco* at the hotel from my room, thus the letterhead. I continued in *Lima*. The pages grew in number. It was only in *Iquitos*, with the help of my friend, *Pisco*, that I could get to the point."

"The photos you took of *Machu Picchu* are spectacular."

"Thanks. I know. Alex likes them. He was so happy to get there. He's so wonderful to be with. He makes everything so exciting."

"I know it is none of my business, but friendship is one thing, important though it is—and this we have and I hope we always will—but you are still young—and time is quickly passing us by—have you thought of marriage, the possibility of—dare I say it—children, before it's too late?"

Marty was afraid he had gone too far. He felt as if he had blurted it out. Sonia did not look at him. She took her glass brought it up to her mouth and let the rim rest on her lower lip. Both sat quietly. She seemed to be enjoying the fruity aroma of the Sancerre. Marty lost track of time until the telephone rang. He picked it up, listened, hung up. "That was Alex," he said. "He told me he has to meet a client; I shouldn't wait for dinner. You want to have some Chinese?"

Sonia nodded. "Can we have it here?" she said. "I'd rather not run into Alex later at your place."

They went around the corner to the restaurant and ordered take out. When they returned to Marty's office, they ate while Marty talked shop. After they cleared the dishes, Sonia started to speak as if in a dream.

"You know," she said. "How to describe it? Perhaps it's an obsession. Perhaps it is more like dull unquelled emotion, a hunger, an unsatisfied sexual urge, a desire, an expectation, a hope or a wish or a dream; maybe just a combination of all. It's like a low-grade disease that becomes chronic. It is a permanent condition with which one has to learn to live."

Marty didn't know how to respond or even if a response was expected. He remained silent. He wasn't sure he knew what she was alluding to, but he was reluctant to venture an opinion. Desire was not a proper subject for discussion. After a pause she continued.

"A few years ago, I met a man who reminded me of Alex. Not in looks, but in his approach to life. There was something about him, something special. He's a lawyer, well-traveled, knowledgeable in many areas other than law. He's handsome: tall, dark, well-built, athletic. A commanding presence. He likes water; he has an affinity for anything to do with the ocean. I met him in Paris. He convinced me to go with him to Rhodes. He likes the Greek islands. Any island for that matter, but Rhodes is not far from Paris. I was supposed to be working on developing an outline for a study on—it doesn't matter. I decided it could wait. I went with him. I may have started off on the wrong foot because I insisted on paying my own way. It could have been foolish on my part because he doesn't need a contribution from me. Alex and I, when we first traveled together, always split expenses, although he no longer permits me to do so because, as he says, I am not as well paid as he. But this was not Alex."

Marty replenished her wine and Sonia took a sip. "I knew," she said, "that the hotel would present a problem. We spent a couple of days in Athens. We took two rooms, but he wasn't happy. When we arrived at the *Hotel des Roses* in Rhodes, we were offered a suite. I found it hard to insist on a separate room. By that time, I thought I might not want it. There was something about this man that kept bringing Alex to mind. I guess, you could say, I was hungry. After we checked in, he was eager to go for a swim. We took a taxi which took us to a cove he knew. Although it was rocky, the water was translucent, light blue, gentle. We put on goggles and swam. We had the entire place to ourselves. It was paradise. Dinner at the hotel restaurant, overlooking the ocean, was excellent. I am running out of adjectives to describe the prelude. But the postlude, to compensate, needs none.

"Yes. After dinner we danced and drank champagne. The moon shone over the ocean. It was peaceful and relaxing. All the right things were in place. It was nothing like *Puno*, as you can imagine. In *Puno* I needed no romantic setting. In Rhodes nothing would do, even if it was perfect in every way. Eventually, we went up to our suite. I did not resist. My heavens, I couldn't have asked for a more beautiful body so well-endowed by nature to satisfy me. And he did. But, although I closed my eyes and pretended he was Alex, he wasn't.

"I still see him occasionally. You may guess who he is. I won't tell you. He realized I was responding mechanically. He guessed there was somebody else. I could not deny it. You see, I did try, but I can't get Alex out of my system even if I know it will never be. Alex is as good as married to you. He will never be mine. I know it. *Puno* confirmed it. I can't help it."

Marty sipped his wine. If she had it to lose, she had written. Yes, she had, if not then sometime earlier accompanying Alex on any one of his business trips, of that he was certain, but to what end? "I wish it had worked out," he said.

Sonia had an impish look. Marty felt as if she had put him under a microscope. "I guess I could've compromised. I don't know if I would've made him happy, especially since he sensed I held back. I would've had to work hard to convince him it wasn't true. I would've had to train myself to fake it. Maybe with time, because we have so much in common, sex would've mattered less. But I couldn't because it would be dishonest. Can one build a relationship on dishonesty? I don't think so."

Marty got up. He rinsed the glasses. He dried them. He put them away in the bottom drawer of his desk. The bottle went into the wastebasket. He embraced Sonia. He kissed her on her forehead. She held on to him, afraid to let go. He knew where the truth lay. She all but confessed it. It hid in her letter. He did not, could not acknowledge that he knew, not to Sonia, not to Alex. What cluttered his mind was the sudden realization that Sonia had married herself to Alex and indirectly to him, a fact that could never be made public. This was the trio they fine-tuned in the years since they met in Paris.

* * * * *

Books on 95 grew like an oak. It put down roots, bore through to the second floor where its trunk solidified and eventually managed to push branches into every crevice of the third floor.

Marty bought the building. A few years later, summer found Sonia in France. Alex had switched jobs to join a firm of management consultants with a branch office in Paris, which is where he was on special assignment. Marty imported books from France but rarely set foot in the country. He minded the store. He was having fun. He was looking forward to living with Alex in a home where both unlocked the same door with the same key. In the post-Stonewall era of gay liberation their wish for a conventional housing arrangement had become acceptable. Since Alex's parents had died, any reason to hide their relationship similarly vanished. He scoured the city for an apartment, preferring the area around the Village and to the South of Houston. Although he would have liked a two-bedroom home, which would have provided for a separate music *cum* library room, he balked at the expense. Eventually he settled on a stunning one-bedroom co-op with a terrace overlooking Gramercy Park and rushed home to call Alex before committing to the purchase.

Having rushed home and up the stairs, he found himself facing a stranger standing in front of Alex's door. An intruder? A break-in? Marty felt his body become rigid as it prepared for defense. An unfamiliar someone looking for Alex was improbable. The person standing in front of him was young, tall, athletic, thick black hair, attractive. After a moment, he determined he did not present a physical threat and let his instinct for politeness prevail. "May I help you?" Marty said.

"I'm looking for paper to write."

"How did you get in the door?"

"The landlord."

Marty was confused. The front door is always locked. The landlord would have to verge on insanity to casually let a stranger in to write a note to a tenant who he knew was away. How could he gauge what the man's intentions were, particularly given the number of break-ins and muggings in the city? Marty wondered what kind of story he made up to gain entry.

"I apologize for being nosy, but what did you tell him? You must understand that in New York we don't casually let strangers in."

"Sorry I frightened you. I'm an old pal. A friend. We had a date 'bout two weeks ago. Never showed. Never came by to explain. Didn't telephone. So, I worried. So, I came by. I rang, rang, rang his office, but nothing. He's away. When he's here, he answers. But I don't come by and won't call home. The landlord, too, said he's away, but didn't know when he's back. I didn't want him to see me write. I asked him to let me come and slip it under the door. I found I don't have paper. I'm in trouble. Can you help?"

Alex had a what? With an "old pal 'bout two weeks ago?" That's a date, isn't it? Did Marty hear right? He must have. That's what he said. His body adjusted from defense against physical attack to resisting emotional betrayal. Alex was playing, was he? Innocent little games he once called them. Innocent still so many years later was hard to believe. He must have graduated to complex games. The player before him did not seem to be one to indulge in simple games. The note, yes, we'll see the note, eventually. Patience, wait, later, you'll figure it out. Get the man out first. Concentrate on what's important, now. Get rid of him. Fast.

Yet Marty couldn't help but admire the young man. He could be described as sleazily elegant. And he told a likely story. Although he had a hard time believing it, there it was. Alex did have good taste. There was no way he could let the boy, as that is what he considered him to be, look through his door, while he fetched paper. Unless he ran in first to hide his photograph with Alex in front of Books on 95 mounted in the silver frame on the side table by the couch. Much too revealing. And where else could the boy sit and write except on the couch? No way could he go inside. No way could he intimate what his relationship was to Alex. His mind was a jumble. He stood for what he thought was forever when it occurred to him, but I do have paper. I have a wad in my pocket. It is nothing more than the small pad on which I have been jotting down all the information about the apartment.

Marty put his hand in his Mackintosh pocket and took out the pad of paper. He carefully removed the top pages with his notes and handed it to the young man. Marty stood aside to give privacy its due, in full knowledge that eventually he would enter Alex's apartment and read at leisure what the scribe was composing.

When he finished, the young man smiled at Marty, bent down, leaned on one knee and carefully pushed the pieces of paper under the door. He stood and gracefully bowed to Marty, his way of thanking him.

"Any idea when he's back?"

"Not really. For all I know he is gone away a week or a month or a year. I just live across the hall." Marty was spitting bile.

"Would you let him know, if you see him, I came by? Name's Billy. He'll know."

Billy started down. Marty followed to make sure he closed the door behind him. When he heard it slam shut, Marty climbed back to the landing and sat down on the top step with his head in his hands. He wanted to scream to the world but held it in, afraid he'd frighten the neighbors. He was reminded to go into the apartment when he heard the landlord fussing with the garbage cans outside and realized he had been sitting for hours. Earlier he had intended to reach Alex; now it was late, besides which he had nothing to say.

The next morning Marty asked Ben to tell Alex and Sonia he wasn't available to talk if they called. In the apartment he stopped answering the telephone. His friends could reach him through the store where Ben would monitor his calls. After a few days Alex tried to reach him through the store; Sonia's call followed almost immediately. If they insisted to know where he was, Ben was to say he was in Mexico, although he had not taken a vacation for more than a long weekend since he opened the store. They both got the same story. Marty hoped they would soon realize he did not want to talk to either. He rang the real-estate agent, as promised, ready to tell him he regretted it wouldn't work because he needed two bedrooms. When he heard the apartment was no longer available before he uttered even one word, the dream he had of living with Alex as a family shattered.

Right before Alex returned, Marty moved to the store. He placed a cot in the storeroom behind his office, which, with the bathroom and kitchen he had retained when converting the brownstone, would be comfortable enough. Marty made sure Alex found all doors closed to him. After he finished work there would be no Marty in the apartment and no answer to the bell after the store closed. During business hours, Ben would bar the way explaining, if asked, that Marty was away in Mexico, but he had no idea for how long. Marty built a bunker around himself that Alex could not penetrate.

When Sonia returned a few weeks after Alex, she outmaneuvered Marty and dragged him to a bar on Broadway.

"Why a bar, Sonia? I don't feel like drinking."

"You'll have a Scotch. I'll have a martini. You'll want it when I'm finished. Besides which, this is the only place I can think of where we are assured not to run into Alex."

Marty wasn't talking. Maybe he wasn't willing to listen either. He hadn't made up his mind. There was nothing he wanted to hear and less to say. Certainly nothing concerning Alex. He would be glad of whatever Sonia had to tell him about her work, about Paris, about anything except ... If he wasn't pleased with the conversation, he was walking out. He would, if he had to, but at the same time he did not want to lose her. He held onto the cold, sweaty glass as if it were his last hold on reality.

"What did you do special this summer?" Marty said. It was his attempt at safeguarding the conversation.

"I went to Geneva."

"Why? Any reason?"

"No. Visiting friends. A start off place to see mountains. And glorious mountains they are. And clouds. Lots of photographs of wispy puppy-dog clouds. Some sunsets, too. But then I can't tell which is sunrise and which is sunset when I have the film developed. I should write down where I take every frame, but I don't. Same with clouds. But no matter. Clouds are clouds."

"Were the mountains hospitable?"

"Yes, warmer than you."

"Don't."

"I don't want to. What I want is for you to stop being angry. There is nothing to be angry about."

Marty concentrated on his drink. He was completely engrossed in it. He was adding up the qualities that make Scotch distinctive, but he was befuddled as to why he was drinking at all. He really didn't want to be there.

"Sonia, my love, tell me why are we here?"

"Because I have a story to tell. I want you to hear me out."

"I'll hear you out. After that can I go home? I mean the store."

"All right. You are aware that Alex and I spent a lot of time and money fruitlessly calling you from Paris. Alex returned with a load of work to find your door closed. No Marty. No explanation. The only clues were the set of pots and pans on his kitchen counter and the china, everything for two, on the side table. Any comment?"

"No."

"You are certainly garrulous tonight. I'll continue. When I returned, I found a despondent Alex. He was lonely. He lost weight. He wasn't eating much. He didn't feel like cooking. He couldn't stand your closed door. He didn't want to be alone in his apartment. He asked if he could use my spare room. I didn't have the heart to refuse. And last week he came home before I did, and he did fix a wonderful dinner for me, but he also had a story. He went for a quick drink after work—he left early and walked from Wall Street, at least until he got tired—it was a beautiful day—and ran into an old acquaintance. He was scolded about a date he made before he left for Paris but didn't keep. He didn't explain why. This man tried to reach him without success and finally left a long note, which he slipped under the door of his apartment. He was surprised he had not heard from him. Had he not seen it? Alex, stunned, asked him how he managed to get up to the apartment. The landlord and neighbor across the way facilitated his efforts—not his exact words. He was proud of the ease with which it was accomplished. Alex didn't tell me how he got out of admitting he didn't know anything about a note. Alex figured you saw it. You read it. You walked out. I decided you would never give up the only other thing that you cherish: your bookshop. You have never ever gone on vacation since it opened, not since you and I were together in Paris. When was it? Late 60s? Mexico? Don't make me laugh. You have never expressed any interest. You had to be here. I came by after 10 tonight. I crawled around the back. I eventually saw a crack of light. I threw one rock, another rock, a third on the window. I was running out of rocks. You were surprised to hear noise. You came to the window. I suppose you never open it, the way it creaked as you forced it open. Now drink."

Marty raised his glass to Sonia. "To my favorite gumshoe, a Sam Spade impersonator," he said. "Great powers of deduction, in addition to great beauty."

"Thanks for the compliment. That's not what I want. I want peace among the three of us. How do we get from here to there?"

"We don't."

"You have to give me a reason."

"I may have to get drunk to invent one. In my sober state, I don't see why I should."

Marty played with the empty glass. He heard Sonia summon the bartender and order a double Scotch on the rocks for him and a soda for herself. "I don't drink by myself, especially when I don't really feel like drinking," he interjected. He was tired but not tired enough not to be rebellious.

A double Scotch and a martini appeared before them. "Sonia, why? I had thought of walking out if you led me in a direction I don't want to go. But I can't do it, not in the middle of the night."

"What was in the note?"

"With due respect, none of your business. It's between Alex and me."

"May I guess?"

"It's a free country."

"Alex screwed around."

"You said it. I didn't. Mind the language, though. Not appropriate, Professor."

"Let's finish our drinks. I'll take a taxi home. You can go back to the apartment. I'll have to figure something out. Alex can't stay with me forever. I'm not a natural born peacemaker, but I'll try to learn a few techniques. I hope you'll let me try."

Marty drank. Sonia drank. Marty couldn't fathom what her thoughts could be in the circumstances. She had feelings. He was certain she had feelings for Alex. He imagined she might resent Billy as much as he did. If she would forgive Alex, he wasn't sure he could. The note he read was a love letter. In the age of AIDS how could Alex have strayed with a boy he couldn't know much about, a kid probably trying to earn a living? Sonia was not a country girl unaware of what was going on in the world. He couldn't get himself to talk to her about AIDS and his worry about what it could mean for him and Alex. She was safe, at least he hoped so. It comforted him to think so, but it didn't make it any easier.

"Let's take you home," Marty said.

Marty got in a taxi with Sonia. He was uneasy and wasn't prepared to trust a taxi driver to take her home. He geared himself to face Alex who he was convinced would be told of their encounter first thing in the morning. He went to the apartment instead of his precious Books on 95.

The week went by with no Alex. It was not until Sunday morning that he heard the familiar clunk, clunk, clunk up the stairs. Marty was grateful it was a day when both were free. The moment he heard the footsteps on the landing, he opened the door enough to stick his head out to say, "I assume you have come for the note from Billy?"

"No." Alex pushed the door open. "No hug? No how are you?"

"The note. You don't want it? It's quite a love note. Must have been great sex to elicit such response—especially from somebody whose vocabulary is..."

"Please don't."

"I'll get it. Take it and leave."

Alex pushed his way in. He sat on the couch. "Don't. I come to make peace. Offer me a cup of coffee."

"I'll offer you the door."

"Marty, this isn't like you. Please hear me out."

"Nothing to hear."

"Yes, there is. We've been together, how long, some thirty something when I include our college years. All right, I made a mistake. I erred. I admit it. Can I not be forgiven? If I were a Catholic, I could go to confession and ask for absolution for my sins. Are you less compassionate than a parish priest? I don't believe it is not within you to forgive. Will you?"

Marty became so angry he felt only bile would sputter out of his mouth. In pain, he managed to spit out, "Please get out." The "please" reverberated in his mind as an avoidable civility he could no longer retract.

"I'll go. There is no talking to an angry man. I love you. Remember I have never loved anyone else."

Marty closed the door behind him and crumpled onto the floor. For the first time since his youth, when he trained himself not to cry, he did. He stretched out on the carpet and eventually fell asleep. The telephone woke him. He got up from the floor in a daze and picked it up automatically. It was Sonia. She was at the payphone on the corner across the street worried because he wasn't opening the downstairs door when she rang his bell. She wanted to know why he wasn't letting her in. He couldn't answer. He wasn't sure if he had or hadn't heard it. In his sleep he could have been having a dream and in his dream world he could have opted to ignore it. Yes, she was certain he was there. That's why she let the telephone ring on until he answered. She wanted to come up. She was so assertive he had no choice but to give in. He stood by the telephone in a daze and waited a few minutes for her to cross the street before he buzzed her in.

"Why are you here?"

"Because a little bird twittered words of advice in my ear. The little bird suggested I not rush. I waited. Here I am."

"That's not a reason."

"Let me think. How about if I say I'm here because I love you."

"You're a liar. You know it isn't true. The love of your life is Alex."

"Did anger sever your tongue from your brain? I do love you." Sonia walked towards the bathroom, stood for a moment as if preparing to enter and instead turned around. "Don't lash out at me. Don't aim to hurt me because you are hurt. It doesn't become you." She came up to him taking a stand as if to lecture. "Besides, you know it isn't true. You're old enough to know sexual attraction and love may not necessarily equate." Sonia surveyed the room.

"What are you looking at?"

"I'm looking at you. I'm looking at the dirty dishes in the sink, at the unfinished breakfast." Marty saw what Sonia saw and shrugged. He felt a mess. "I have a suggestion. Go wash your face, put on a clean shirt and a pair of walking shoes while I clean up the kitchen. We'll go for a stroll in Central Park. The sun is shining in case you haven't noticed."

Marty was undecided, unable to sort himself out. Take the path of least resistance, he told himself. Leave this stifling room. But is she telling the truth, he wondered, could it really be true she doesn't want Alex? If he were in her place, he wouldn't settle for half a loaf. It's all or nothing. The lyrics of that old popular song started going through his head. What was it? "All or nothing at all / Half a loaf never appealed to me / If something or other never could yield to me...something, something then I'd rather have nothing at all." The lyrics felt wrong. It couldn't have been about bread. Was "love" the word he was avoiding? That was his dilemma, wasn't it? What did he want? It wasn't nothing, was it? But he certainly wasn't having all. What about something? Don't know was his response. Sonia is lucky. If she had wanted Alex, it was then, perhaps no longer now. Otherwise why was she here? He washed his face. He started to hum.

"What are you humming?" said Sonia.

"It's from long ago. I can't remember the words."

Marty hoped she would not respond. She had agreed to part of a loaf, if that much. All was not in the realm of possibility. Probably nothing was not accurate either. Why bring it up now? They walked up 93rd Street to enter the park. They crossed the bridal path and the promenading Sunday riders. They went over to the tennis courts to watch the players, and when boredom set in, they cut across to the North Gate House and the path circumvallating the reservoir. The ducks were out, geese flew overhead, the blue jays squawked, the herons strutted on the opposite shore. The scent of autumn was in the air, although the trees had not yet lost their late summer feathery fullness. A stream of fast walkers and joggers came towards them. Marty relaxed. Sonia took his hand and held it tight. Marty was glad Sonia did not pry. As they approached the South Gate House, Sonia veered toward the Metropolitan Museum. They took the path by Cleopatra's Needle and exited from the park on 79th Street and Fifth Avenue. They admired the stands of street venders crowding in front of the grand neo-classical façade as they passed by before mounting the stairs to the museum.

Without a clear plan, they found themselves in the Greek and Roman Hall. Marty heard Sonia break the silence between them as through a fog. They were the first words either had uttered since leaving the apartment, and strange words they were. "Why do you suppose the male statues surrounding us have such small penises?"

"Haven't noticed. Let's see." He looked up and down the parade of nude statuary that flanked either side of the walkway through the rectangular room and proceeded to walk around each and every male hovering over him. She was right. "Why indeed?" he said.

"Come to think of it. It isn't only the Greeks and the Romans. Let's consider Michelangelo's *David*, in Florence. Remember?"

"I wonder, could there have been a convention, perhaps, to make it invisible, or nearly so. Most people are unaware. Our ideal rests on a perfect torso, the drape of the toga, the musculature, the pose to showcase the structure of the body. The penis is insignificant. Didn't the Greeks adjust human reality to the ideal? Most humans do not have perfect features, but they were sculpted as if they did. But a small penis as an ideal? Sounds perverted to me. Want to do a survey and assess the response?"

"I think we'll be charged with disturbing the peace, unruly conduct, promoting pornography, or some such." Sonia acted shocked at the suggestion.

"Weird, isn't it? In real life neither the Romans nor the Greeks nor the Italians seem to have suffered. Fecund they certainly were. Healthy sex lives they all led. Read any Catullus lately?"

"Marty, so you know Catullus, do you? Do you mean to tell me you carry his poems in the store? Pornography! I'm surprised at you."

Marty laughed. "Let's go to where the view is more sedate. How about the medieval hall?"

Soon they found themselves surrounded by sculpture of another age, different sensibility. Marty stopped by a standing virgin and child, French 14th Century. "Is it a child? Looks like a little old man. Funny expression: could be a smirk or a smile. Why does a child on a painting or an icon or a carving look so unchildlike? To me, most resemble lecherous, little, old men, grabbing at her veil or her belt. Any idea?"

"Not my field. Let's go find El Greco's *View of Toledo*. He should cheer us up. All this sex is depressing."

"Sorry the Met doesn't have Vermeer's *View of Delft*. I could stand a disquisition on the little yellow spot. Pure Proust. I can't imagine we would encounter a similar problem in El Greco. Maybe we could invent one. It's the character Bergotte, isn't it, who when he studied the Vermeer noted the yellow patch? Scholars have been arguing ever since, haven't they, wondering which of the three patches he refers to?"

Marty winked at Sonia and half smiled. He figured the last thing on which she would want to hold forth that moment is what Proust intended. "I suggest we move on," he said. "Straight across around Third Avenue, I think, there's a good Czech restaurant. I haven't been there in a long while, but if we get there soon, we might be able to get a table without waiting. I'm a bit peckish. Afterwards, if you don't mind, I would like to drop you off and go home. I'm weary, a comfortable weariness, thanks to you."

Marty felt Sonia grab his hand. Not one to waste words, he knew she was pleased he was behaving more like himself. He bent over and kissed her on the head. At the restaurant, he ate, drank and talked with the uncanny awareness of the slow passage of time. The emptiness inside him did not dispel. He couldn't be bothered to wait for a bus so he walked home from her apartment through the park, not a very safe thing to do after dark, but he didn't care. He was relieved to be alone in familiar surroundings at the end of a long day.

The next morning Marty ran into the landlord who gave his opinion, unasked, how awful it must be for a person to travel continuously because of a job. He himself, he said, liked to stay home. No argument. How he knew Alex was gone, he didn't say. Marty figured Sonia would know why he left suddenly, but he wasn't curious enough to inquire. He could imagine Alex browsing for books for him on the stalls on the Seine. Habit is ingrained. He always does.

Well, not this time, not after recent events. But it's his way to relax when he is alone. In summer with Sonia, it's different. She accompanies him when one of his colleagues invites him home for dinner, a rare event once in a French household but more common now. Together they go everywhere. She is his pal, his companion, his favorite lady. When he is alone, he gets bored. Marty decides to worry. An Alex alone without Sonia, an Alex who no longer has Marty, will he look for young boys? Has he always been on the lookout? Marty stop it. It's not your worry. How can you ever know what Alex does when he is by himself? Consider what he did coming home to you every night? He found himself a Billy. Maybe Alex is doing nothing more than moping in Paris. He can't reach Marty. Marty threw him out, but he can't live by himself. Is he seeing a psychiatrist, a psychoanalyst, a counselor of some sort to figure out how to get Marty back? What can he do to reach Marty? Maybe Alex is as unhappy as Marty is. Marty fiddles no melody he knows; he's lost.

"Marty are you there?" It was Sonia calling late at night. "I have tickets to the opera this Thursday. Are you coming with me?"

"What is it?"

"Lulu."

"It'll cheer me up. I love Lulu. She skewers her men in style. She, sadly, gets her comeuppance, though, when Jack the Ripper does her in, doesn't he?"

"You can put pins in Lulu imagining her as Alex. I'll keep mum about it."

Marty came home late, a week after the Lulu evening, and heard music across the landing. The door was closed. Sonia must have gotten tired of the permanent guest in her study. Alex may have decided it was time to return to the place for which he paid rent. Tomorrow is another day.

Both doors remained closed, although the landing often reverberated with music. With no Alex to help, Marty got into the habit of working on his accounts after store hours. But one night he also wrote a note, which read: "Would you come for coffee tonight when I come home, say, about nine?" He was contemplating slipping it under the door in the morning when he left for work. When the time came he realized, however, Alex had gone before him, so he lost his nerve and did nothing. Phantoms avoiding each other in the penumbra of their lives was no solution. He rewrote the note to read, "Would you come for coffee and cake tomorrow night? I will try to make it early, say, about eight? He signed it with a simple initial. It took him another week before he slipped it under Alex's door, last thing at night before turning in. In the morning a piece of paper appeared with a simple "Yes" under his door. No signature.

Marty fussed all day about cake. A matter of little consequence became an issue. He ended up making time to leave the store, which he did only in emergencies, to grab a taxi to take him to the East Side to *Dumas*, the

French pastry shop on Madison Avenue. He extravagantly asked the driver to wait. He returned the proud owner of apple tarts a and petit-fours, 24 pieces altogether, enough for a party of at least six.

Coffee was ready when Alex gently knocked on the open door. The cakes, the majority in reserve in the box, were decorously displayed on the coffee table. Marty heard the second-act music of Tristan softly from across the landing. He poured coffee. Black, no sugar, for Alex. He handed him the cup and saucer and poured himself a half-cup and sat down.

Alex helped himself. "My favorite apple pie," he said. "Nobody makes tarts like the French." He held one up in his hand to admire and to enjoy its aroma. He took a bite.

"Sorry, I forgot." Marty said, embarrassed, "I forgot plates and forks." Who would have thought it would be the absence of plates and cutlery that would successfully mediate between them? Alex took another apple tart not waiting for a plate. Marty took a petit-four, because it could be held without dirtying fingers.

Marty munched on his cake. He did not look at Alex. When he finished, he raised his eyes and was met by Alex staring at him. He did not resist when Alex sidled up to him to cradle him in his arms. Give in—go on—that's what you want. Yes, but is it what I want after what he did? Forgive, go on. Forget—no never, another voice rose up in Marty to command. But Marty did give in, a little at a time. Alex kissed him once and again and then without stopping unzipped his pants and removed his briefs. Alex got him up so he could move the furniture and open the couch. Marty let Alex pull him into bed. He let himself be loved. He couldn't help himself and loved back. His body relaxed and gave in. He was carried into that unconscious, mysterious land where two minds, two hearts and whatever else constitutes their being become as entwined as their bodies. He had missed Alex and was happy. Had Alex missed him? After he uncoiled his body from Alex's, and rested on his back, he couldn't help but wonder if it was the same with Billy; he would have liked to know, but didn't dare ask. Such thoughts destroyed his mood and broke the spell.

Marty was relieved Alex was back. He didn't like war so he permitted himself to accept a truce. He was trying to remember what he knew about war and what became of a truce. Often it was broken. He pondered the steps required to lead to peace. He ached. What could have made Alex do it? Was it the first time? Just the last time? Was it that Billy's hair was as black as his used to be before it was diluted by a network of white strands? But then Alex, once pure blond, was a paler blond because of the admixture of white, and therefore appeared younger—though the network of wrinkles and incipient jowls could not help but confirm his maturity. Marty couldn't help but think of him as an "Old Goat". Maybe I wouldn't be so hurt, Marty scolded himself, if only Billy were a little older. Older or younger, no matter. No, Marty, you are not ready to forget. He postponed the discussion. First what was to be done with those cakes? Only three had been eaten. Freeze them; replace the ice-cube trays with petits fours, he commanded himself. Damn these half-size refrigerators. So many cakes, so little space. Squeeze them in.

It was a couple of weeks before Marty invited Sonia to help finish the cakes. She brought yellow roses. "I like flowers in a room. They bring cheer. Look at your cakes,

Marty. Did you not ask Dumas if they had madeleine*s*? If we had them, we could play to see what memories they would trigger. But you didn't think of it. Shame on you. I've gone into games, children's games and nursery rhymes; I've gone into my childhood."

"What kind of games?" Marty asked.

"Listen:

Hey, diddle, diddle,
The cat and the fiddle,
The cow jumped over the moon;
The little dog laughed
To see such sport,
And the dish ran away with the spoon.

"Charming," said Marty. "Now explain."

"Easy. I'm the little dog who witnessed the sport. Translation. You and Alex at odds. And I hope the game between you is over. You, I hope, are the dish that runs away with Alex, the spoon. And live happily ever after."

Marty reminded himself, no it was not a spoon, it was a fork.

* * * * *

Martinis were the vogue in the household, vodka martinis that is, but according to a formula Alex and Sonia devised. The standard cocktail consists of extra-dry vermouth-infused vodka, but Punt e Mes, a bittersweet vermouth aperitif Alex discovered in Italy, had replaced the Stock vermouth in their preferred drink. With an added sliver of lemon peel, it made a delicious drink oozing a very individual kind of perfume. Marty did not change his habits. He stuck to Scotch. The studios had been replaced by a one-bedroom condominium. Technically, according to the trade, a convertible two-bedroom. That accounted for two bathrooms plus the dining area, which adjoined the kitchen and could, if desired, be transformed into the said second bedroom. And that space so perfect for its initial function is what had attracted Alex and Marty. The apartment was furthermore registered jointly in both their names as tenants in common.

Alex, having let himself in, came into the kitchen after hanging up his coat in the foyer closet. As Marty was fussing with dinner, he handed him his Scotch. His own drink, he prepared meticulously, taking time to make it just as he liked it, with only a whiff of vermouth. "Sonia is home. She came back yesterday," Alex said. "I've invited her for dinner tomorrow."

Marty turned from the stove where he had been adding mushrooms to the chicken in wine sauce and said, "Suppose you'll do the cooking?"

"No. Can't. Business." Alex turned to Marty to make sure he took note of the seriousness of his predicament. The face he showed Marty was devoid of any expression. Marty was forced to laugh. He assumed Alex had been saddled with a meeting in which he would rather not participate. "All right. Peace," he said. "How are we going to manage?"

"You know the answer; why ask?"

"I can only think of our version of fast food. I'll put it out when I get home. You tell Sonia it will be a meager repast, early 1950's French style, about 9:00 o'clock or a little after."

Marty had a new shipment of books to sort. It was work he preferred to do after the shop closed. Sometimes, if he did not feel the need to peruse each individually, he would ask Ben to work with him. This time, however, he had decided to work alone. That is why he did not expect to be home in time to make dinner at the normal 6:00 or so. He did not find it necessary to explain any of this to Alex because Alex knew his habits. Yet, he seemed oblivious. No, not really. Caring Alex was never unmindful. He seemed distant, unconcerned, possibly troubled, maybe disturbed. Yet Marty sensed Alex was uneasy, but whatever the cause the source eluded him.

As it happened, Marty finished sorting and stacking books a bit earlier than anticipated and got home more than half an hour before Sonia was due. He rang the doorbell expecting Alex to rush to help with the groceries. No answer. Nobody home. How late could his meeting have dragged on? A night meeting? Unusual. Marty brought the bags into the kitchen and like a whirlwind set the table, prepared scrod filets for baking, put potatoes in the oven, set vegetables in the microwave, put together the salad of greens, shoved the ice cream into the freezer, made himself a drink, changed his clothes, and like a gentleman of leisure sat down in the living room to await his guests. The wide-screen television flickered with the sound off. The question of why Alex was so late droned on. He had offered no reason why he could not, at least, be home before Sonia. There was no voicemail message. The doorbell clanged to bring an end to his ruminating. Marty ran to open the door.

"Give me a hug," Sonia said. She wrapped her arms around Marty pulling him gently down.

While Sonia fixed her hair in the foyer mirror, he hung her coat in the closet. Marty stopped to admire the stunning figure. Forty plus years after they met she was still a good looking blond, albeit the blond had become blended into gray. She was wearing a pantsuit—a dark blue suit that was becoming for an elegant lady with a figure still able to show it off in the sixth decade of her life. She had a small package, which she passed on to him but which he absentmindedly put aside, having expected to see Alex at the door. Sonia retrieved it and thrust it again into his hand. "A small present for you. From Morocco."

Marty opened it and out came what his fingers informed him was leather but folded like origami. The design of alternating red and black octagons was a feast for the eyes. The softness of the leather on the hand was caressing. He examined it.

"Don't look so puzzled," Sonia said. "It serves the same purpose as a footstool. You rest your feet on it. Set it in front of your favorite armchair. You who stand most of the day can surely use an object like this. Before you can, however, you have to unfold it, stuff it with whatever you wish—newspaper will do—that's what I did—lace it up, and there you are, you have created a useful art object."

Sonia walked around the apartment inspecting the premises. "Where's Alex?" she asked, expecting him to appear from behind the CD player or the audio system with speakers in every room that had replaced the old KLH. She looked in the bedroom before returning to the living room. "Why no music? Is he in the bathroom?"

"No. He didn't warn me he would be this late."

Marty disappeared in the kitchen. He was worried. True, Sonia was a bit early and it wasn't quite 9:00 o'clock.

But Alex, the host, should be home to receive his guest. He made a Punt e Mes martini for Sonia and refilled his Scotch and brought them on coasters to the cocktail table by the couch. He sat down next to her.

Both were silent, a comforting silence. Marty didn't mind, but it was not like her. She was an articulate lady, rarely at a loss for words. She had been gone all summer and that she had no stories to tell was odd. He didn't question her, his mind still mulling over Alex.

"What's with Alex? Sonia said.

Marty was shaken. Could she be reading his mind? He said, "What do you mean?"

"A question in response to a question is a good way to get nowhere." She paused. Marty sensed she was gathering her thoughts. "Alex behaves oddly sometimes, in my eyes anyway. That's what troubles me."

"No, I'm not playing," he said. "What bothers me is that he did not warn me he was going to be so late. All he said was that he couldn't make dinner. I don't understand why he isn't here."

"I'm not concerned about his being late. It's his general behavior lately."

"You've been away all summer. You just came back. You haven't seen him all this time because he didn't go to Paris this year. Since when have you been troubled?"

"No, it's not that." Sonia looked expectantly at Marty. He held back. He wasn't prepared to share his own unease with her because it was so nebulous. Since the Billy incident he and Alex had fallen into the habit of giving each other more freedom. He couldn't therefore account for all his actions, if one ever could for another human being. He waited to hear what Sonia had in mind.

"I don't know how to put it," she said. "It's something intangible. Alex was always warm. I can't say cuddly, because neither of you is cuddly. But he was never remote, removed, disconnected. I mean physically. It's as if he doesn't want to be touched. I felt it last winter and it was worse in the spring. I can't quite figure it out."

Marty ignored sex. He was worried that Alex had become emotionally distant whereas Sonia touched on the physical. Maybe both were right. Yes, sex. In the recent past, he couldn't think of when. But then, he had been busy to the point of exhaustion and usually went straight to bed. Not a subject to be shared, particularly not with Sonia. One normally doesn't talk to friends about beds, does one? Except, come to think of it, Sonia and Alex's series of allegedly no-sex beds. No, not a subject for discussion.

"For many a summer," Sonia said. "Alex always made time; he always found a week or two to join me in Paris. Not this year. He surely knows I would have ..."

The sound of keys jangling at the door reverberated. Sonia never finished her sentence. Marty figured the intended allusion must have been to a Morocco visit she would have foregone if on the one hand and if Alex on the other and so on. Marty was relieved that that part of the conversation had come to an end. Alex walked into the living room cheerfully as if he were the Pied Piper of Hamelin ready to lead a starved crew to a late repast.

Sonia eagerly jumped up from the sofa, ran towards Alex and leaped up, her arms stretched upwards. Alex held her as she hung on to his neck and gave him a big kiss. He laughed joyfully. "Welcome home, our happy wanderer," he said. He hugged her and gently put her down.

Marty gave Alex his martini and disappeared into the kitchen. Sonia went into the guest bathroom. Alex joined Marty in the kitchen and put on a front of being cheerful. No apologies for being late. No physical greeting to him and probably none to Sonia if she hadn't embraced him. He couldn't believe Alex had not pecked at her cheek in return. Marty announced dinner after the few minutes it took for the fish to cook and the baked potatoes, the salad and vegetables to be prepared.

Alex in the meantime had busied himself opening a bottle of Chablis. At the table, he raised his glass. "A toast to our guest. We welcome her and wish her success in the coming year at school and on her new book."

Marty concentrated on the fish. Alex was putting on an act. He was hyperactive. What could it be? Work? No reason. Marty would have known if anything unusual had occurred. He certainly had not been fired. There was that odd meeting tonight. He had not been promoted, but he couldn't be for he was already partner. He wasn't straying, not that he knew. Morocco would be a good distraction. "Can you tell us about your North African adventure now that we are all together?" Marty said.

Sonia started her tale, but Marty didn't pay attention. He vaguely heard how it all started with a new friend whom she accompanied, but he did perk up at the reference to the city of Casablanca because they were talking about the film. This one in particular was part of their youth, his youth, to the extent that he had seen it so many times it was embedded in memory.

"You mean did I find Rick's?" Sonia said. "Has anybody heard of Rick's? Is that what you're asking?"

Alex made sure all their glasses were full before he raised his and with a twinkle in his eye looked directly at Sonia and said, "Here's looking at you, kid." He took a sip. A big smile spread over his face.

Sonia raised her glass in turn. She was radiant. Slowly her face grew grave, the corners of her mouth turned down. "Sorry. No Rick's. It's a lively town. Casbah very much like the one in that Casablanca, but no Rick's. No Elsa either. Mind you, if you go with a tour the chances are that any old café you pass will be pointed out as the original Rick's. Probably nobody told the guides—and even if they were told they probably wouldn't listen—that the original Rick's was constructed on a Hollywood sound stage to resemble a swanky 1940s American nightclub, swing band, black performer and all. I think it was the wrong, albeit the real, Casablanca I visited. But let me tell you about Rabat. There is an old fort by the sea. Next time we get together at my place I'll remember to show you the photo my friend took. You won't believe what you'll see. It was quite cloudy. I was standing by the parapet when the clouds opened up and the sun came through. The rays emerged star-like straight onto the ocean and sparkled in the water. There I am with this incredible backdrop. Never take a picture aiming at the sun is the standard instruction. She did. With my camera. And it came out. It has turned into an interesting study in grays, blacks and every shade in between including white. I love it."

Marty observed Alex. He seemed curiously detached while at the same time giving his full attention to Sonia and her report on her return to France through Granada and his favorite in Spain, the Alhambra. He vaguely heard Alex expound on the Lion's Garden, the worldly representation of the ideal of paradise in Arab poetry, and Sonia's response, teasing him about perfect symmetry, in this case the perfect symmetry of the perfect dozen lions— those gorgeous lions—supporting the basin of the fountain in the center on their back.

"You'll never let me forget my woolgathering in the *Place des Vosges*, so many years ago, will you, when I questioned, rhetorically, why symmetry is pleasing. Naughty you. But it is pleasing, isn't it?"

"You're fun to tease. But it's an interesting question, particularly there. One is faced by symmetries, for instance in the friezes, in the filigrees, everywhere. With no physical representation permitted, and nothing but repeated patterns in various guises, it is a world of symmetries. A wonderful way to organize the world around us."

Marty felt disconnected. It was a different universe from the reality that gnawed at him. Alex was performing his assigned role, and doing so very well, yet Sonia kept talking as if the Alhambra was all that mattered. In an attempt to steer the conversation away from the earlier trip Sonia had taken with Alex to Granada, Marty asked, "Where is your friend now?"

"In Paris. I'll probably see her when I go back. I did invite her, but she has no reason to come to New York. I don't know if I'll go to Paris next summer. I may just work here in the library. Incidentally, I have something for you, Alex. Marty got his footstool. You get a little incised box to put your cufflinks in. A remembrance from Morocco to say I love you."

Sonia took the small package from her handbag and passed it to Alex. He rose from the table to give her a hug and a kiss and said, "I have seer's eyes to note the simple elegance of the object within without tugging at the beautifully wrapped box. Thanks, my love." Marty stared. He found it hard to hide his surprise at Alex's exaggerated performance. It was unlike him.

Marty offered to make coffee. Sonia got up, shaking her head in response, as it was close to midnight. Alex went to get his coat to accompany her. After they left, Marty rinsed the dishes. He stacked them in the dishwasher because he had no intention of running it so late at night. All the while his conscience was berating him, asking why he had withheld raising his own misgivings about Alex with Sonia. He had no answer other than that he didn't feel like it. He was tired enough not to try to sort it out, and by the time Alex returned Marty was asleep. The next morning Alex was gone before he got up.

That evening Alex announced he was going on a two-week business trip. He was taciturn. Marty figured it was London where he had been involved in consultations of some kind. If the previous evening's meeting had anything to do with it, Marty never learned. He had stopped asking for details unless Alex volunteered, in which case he simply listened. He helped him pack. Alex was not particularly enthusiastic, which Marty resisted interpreting as fatigue in preference to boredom. The excitement that preceded a trip, a trip to anywhere, was missing. Marty although inclined to question opted not to. He saw him off in the morning before leaving for the store. He worried the two weeks he was gone, in spite of frequent notes and the occasional telephone call.

At the end of September Sonia tried to reach Marty at the store several times during the day. Assuming whatever it was could wait, he did not hurry to respond until evening.

"Marty, Marty," she said as if repeating his name would bring instant help. "Alex informed me sometime after noon that he isn't going to the opera tomorrow. I asked if he had talked to you, and he said he hadn't. He didn't say something had come up; he just said he couldn't go. What's going on?"

"Don't know. Just came home and no Alex."

"I rang the office before trying you, and he's not there."

"Why don't I simply meet you at the opera at our seats? I'll get the ticket from him when I see him. Problem solved. Sorry I can't meet you for supper because Ben can't close up. No time for a change of clothes but hopefully enough for a quick bite. I hope it's an opera I can stand and it's worth the effort."

"It's …"

"Don't tell me the 'it's' or the 'with'. I want to be surprised."

Marty was more than upset. He was in no mood to start dinner without Alex. Although it was usually Alex who put on the CDs that filled the apartment with sound, he felt the need for soothing music and put on the familiar third act of Tristan. He sat on the couch in the living room facing the view across the Hudson River to New Jersey. He was so distracted it only provided a backdrop for his unease. He lost track of time. Eventually he heard the usual jangle of keys that preceded the door opening.

"You there?"

"Where do you expect me to be?"

"Why no lights?"

"I'm waiting."

"You're waiting?"

"Yes."

"What are you waiting for?"

"You tell me."

"I'm in no mood for a who's on third sort of comic routine. It was funny for Abbot and Costello. Not now."

"You're in no mood? Neither am I."

"You sound angry."

"I guess I am."

"Sorry."

Marty was perplexed. He could imagine the many things to which this "sorry" could apply—for being late and not giving him warning he would be late, for not getting in touch with him about the opera after talking to Sonia, for taking no responsibility for making dinner, for the standoffishness that bothered Sonia, for his recent general remoteness—but he couldn't point to one among the many.

"I'm sorry, too, but I don't understand what sorry is all about."

"You sound hurt. That's worse," Alex said. "How's your drink?"

"Waiting for you."

Alex went into the kitchen. He turned on the light, made Marty his Scotch, fixed himself straight vodka and came back to the now semi-lit living room.

"Why are you angry, Marty, my love?"

The bit of light washing out from the kitchen allowed Marty to see Alex, see him as if for the first time. He looked wan and tired. He seemed drained, drained of feeling, of emotion. Could he be frightened? His tie flopping, the knot loosened down at his chest, and the top buttons of his shirt unbuttoned produced an unfamiliar image of carelessness. Had he taken the time since he walked in the door to loosen his tie and unbutton his shirt? Could be, but somehow it was doubtful.

"I'll start with the easy one. Why did you tell Sonia you weren't going with her tomorrow and didn't tell me?"

"Guess I forgot."

"Obvious next line: why did you forget?"

Marty heard Alex gulp his drink. He gulped again. Is it so hard to answer? Why was it so difficult? The silence was depressing. He was becoming irritated enough to want to choke him. He was getting ready physically to squeeze the answer out of him. The moment trailed a heavy load up the invisible mountain of time. He heard Alex gulp his drink again. He couldn't sit still any longer. He got up. "I'm going to replenish my drink. Is yours ready?"

"A bit more vodka, please, straight. Maybe some ice, too, please. I'm drinking too much." Alex said. As an afterthought, he added, "Thank you."

Marty was in no hurry. It was almost as if he were reluctant to return to the living room. He puttered in the kitchen. He took out the defrosting steaks and set them out ready to broil. He set the side dishes on the counter. Before he went back, he put potatoes to cook on the stove. He reminded himself to set the timer before going to Alex with drinks in hand. All the while his mind was churning with questions. Why was he drinking plain vodka? Too lazy to take out the Punt e Mes? And no lemon sliver? Why? The lemons are in the fridge. In so much of a hurry that he skips making what he likes? What's with him? Why is he still standing?

"Do you think this drink will emit an answer?" Marty asked as he handed the glass to Alex.

"Yes, funny man. I have the answer. First, I'll drink a little more. You better drink, too. You'll need it. Here's to better times." His voice was so low Marty at first was uncertain of what he heard.

"To your health," replied Marty.

"Thanks. Just what I need."

Marty returned to his place on the couch. Alex followed him. Marty decided there was no point in badgering him. When Alex would be ready to speak, he would. Both sat looking at the skyline. It was a clear night and the lights sparkled and twinkled and winked across the river as if to say all is well in the world. Marty wanted to believe. Their silence, however, was not the usual silence that exudes comfort among old friends, between aging lovers. It had a slight brittleness that could cause sparks if ignited.

"O.K. I'm ready. But first I want another vodka," Alex said. "I'll refill your drink, too." From the kitchen, he said, "I'm turning these potatoes off. I think they're done. You set a high flame and the timer for much too long. Were you dreaming?"

"I guess I was. Are you hungry?" Marty laughed. It was nervous laughter. Time was moving as slowly as his ability to reason. His instinct to comfort his lover with food overwhelmed his judgment. Bite your tongue, he scolded himself. Stupid thing to say. He was relieved when he heard Alex respond, "No. Now we talk." Alex handed him his drink. He remained standing by the couch.

Marty heard the sound of twirling ice in a glass followed by prolonged silence broken by a big gulp. "I didn't try you after I called Sonia because I completely forgot. It, how to put it, whooshed right out of my mind. I called her minutes before I was called into the examining room because I realized I wasn't fit company to sit through a performance of anything. I had gotten a message in the office in the morning to come in about the results of the blood test. Guess I already knew why. After I heard what the doctor had to say, I just went walking. When I got so tired I couldn't go on, I came home. Here I am."

"How long has this been going on?"

"Oh, I don't know. Six months. Nine months. Maybe longer."

"What's the diagnosis?"

"I have a virus." Marty wasn't amused by the response. To break the silence following that laconic bit of information, he was impelled to ask, "Is it a human virus?" He was not being facetious. The silence harbored the middle word that referred to the deficiency in the immune system. He shivered. Fear of the future the disease augured removed any vestige of anger at the perceived infidelities. He froze.

"Yes, it is a human virus. Maybe animals can also be infected for all I know. You probably guessed the rest. Yes, it concerns the immune system. Yes, I am HIV positive. I made an appointment for you for Friday at 12:30. You should be checked out. You can eat lunch at your desk. All he'll do is take blood. You will probably not be subjected to a long interrogation since the doctor already knows all about you and me. It shouldn't take long. If you can't make it, call and change the appointment. But you better get tested."

Marty closed his eyes and leaned back, turning his face onto the back of the couch. He wanted desperately to block out what Alex had just told him. It couldn't be true. He hadn't heard correctly. Tears welled up in his eyes. The power of speech eluded him. He was still waiting for Alex to come home. He was furious Alex was so late with no warning. He wanted to scream at Alex, but the sound stuck in his throat. He felt numb, abandoned, emotionless, lifeless.

Alex came up from behind and put his arms around Marty. He slowly pirouetted around the couch as he nudged him to sit forward until he could sit next to him. He put his head on Marty's shoulder and locked his arms around him. The two rocked together. When he calmed down, Marty said, "Any idea who infected you?"

"Maybe. I'm the straying one and I should know, but I'm not sure. Not you. You are my loyal companion, a true partner, a forgiving friend. I don't believe you've ever looked at anyone else. But at this point who it is, was, could have been is irrelevant. What I want desperately to know is that you are clear. The doctor says it's possible."

"What made you go for a test? It couldn't have been a regular checkup. You must have felt something was wrong—six months you just said—what happened six months ago? It wasn't six months ago you had blood drawn and only today got the results?"

"How shall I put it? I ran into Billy earlier this year. He didn't look well. He told me he had AIDS. I decided it was too many years ago when he could have infected me. One never knows, but I couldn't rule it out. But we are surrounded with news of AIDS, talk of AIDS, friends with AIDS, plays about AIDS." Alex picked up a bit of fluff from the carpet, played with it and eventually took it into the kitchen to put into the garbage under the sink. When he returned, he continued, "I was frightened, despondent at times, depressed at others. I had a feeling I should check myself out. I should have done something about it, but I couldn't. I was hoping the whole thing would just go away. The doctor's office sent a note—I picked up the mail; you didn't see it—telling me I should come in for a regular physical. The decision was taken out of my hands."

"I wonder. I can't believe you would be capable of it, but with you it's hard to tell. Did you ever sneak off to Cuba, for instance, for some, what shall I say, special entertainment, in Havana?"

"What brings Cuba to mind?"

"When was it you told me you had gone to Cancun for a long weekend? What would a city loving boy like you be doing in a beach-bum paradise like that? It couldn't have been business, real business I mean, could it? I often wondered. You never explained."

"Your sarcasm not appreciated, but maybe, yes, I did, how you put it, sneak off for a few days. I had heard so much about Havana. You may be right. I'll never know. Perhaps I would have been better off being caught by Customs on my way home for trading with the enemy— that would have only involved a hefty fine—rather than possibly returning with a pernicious little bug after what I took to be a lark in a gay paradise. It doesn't feel like that now, I admit."

Alex refilled their drinks and came back unsteadily. Marty wondered how much they had drunk, but couldn't count. He was overcome by desire. The sound in his head resonated with drums beating thump, thump, thump. He looked at Alex longingly as he had the first time so many years ago. He said in a voice so low he wasn't certain he meant for Alex to hear it or only for himself, "Is our only option now to join the order of celibates? I'll have to ask the doctor."

After the Billy incident Marty had managed to persuade Alex that it would be safer if they became a condom family. No not because of Billy, he protested, but in general. Alex eventually came to accept it. Whether he was aware of it or not, that practice helped maintain the truce after their war-like skirmish. He had caught him with his finger in his favorite honey—yes, it's true he tended to think in clichés as Sonia often teased him—and now he had evidence that he liked that particular flavor and had stolen a taste of more than one after the one called Billy but had forgotten to calculate the potential costs. As much as Marty didn't like using those unmentionable objects, he was glad they might save at least one of them, namely himself, from that awful disease. He would soon find out. To his sorrow, Alex did not appreciate the danger and obviously never took care of himself away from Marty. And now there was only Marty to take care of him.

"Here's your drink," Alex said. "What are you muttering about? I couldn't hear."

"What I was saying is that tomorrow is another day. Sonia wants to know why you can't make it—to the opera, I mean. What do I tell her?"

"Just say I have to work late, for a special, urgent job. Maybe skip the urgent. Tonight, too, I was late working on it. That's why I forgot to tell you earlier. You'll cover. You always do. I do love you."

"What I need to know besides that I have your love is the prognosis. What did the doctor say?"

"He tells me that I am for the present in the asymptomatic carrier state. If I am one of the lucky ones, it can go on for quite a while. I guess I'll eventually know things are getting worse when the malaise, fever, rash, and so on start. But what is urgent is to know you are clear, which I pray and hope you are. Next, we'll get separate beds for the bedroom. Tomorrow you go with Sonia. I'll put the ticket out right now, so I won't forget."

When Alex returned, he nestled up to Marty and put his arms around him. Marty sensed Alex was lost in thought. He would have liked to follow him wherever he had gone, but couldn't decide if he would be welcome. Words, however, tumbled out of him.

"I'm ashamed to say, but it's true, I have been selfish, maybe, too involved with my own business, but Sonia did notice you have not been your usual self. She made me aware you have been...." Alex broke in, "Please, promise you'll not tell Sonia, at least not until we have no choice. She must never think AIDS, never. She is never to know."

* * * * *

Without a sound Marty opened the well-oiled door of a private room in the East River Residence. He did not fill the doorway as he once would have with his diminished six-foot plus frame. Nor did a full head of charcoal infused hair having turned silvery white any longer enliven his features. It was the combined action of time and gravity that marked his body. He reflected calm and strength. It was years since he had overcome the depression that almost felled him after he learned he had been spared, and it was only Alex who was HIV positive. His anger abated when he realized that, although illness could have caused their paths in life to diverge, they were bound together perhaps even more tightly than before, be it in a newly discovered dependency. And there was that invisible bond to Sonia, the reason for his visit to the assisted-living facility.

When Marty heard voices, he stopped at the threshold. He surveyed the room, but Sonia was alone. From force of habit he took a moment to admire what was still a handsome woman, as slim as ever, neatly dressed in matching pink slacks and shirt, her gray hair cut short. Sadness overpowered him as he remembered the vibrant woman who had somehow vanished inside a faltering mind. She was talking to herself.

Sonia sat in a bamboo-backed armchair staring through the picture window overlooking the East River. Her eyes were fixed on clouds, nothing but clouds. It was a scene of continuous motion. A lonely stationary single sometimes flitted by; occasionally several came as a group in a jumble or at other times scudded across the eastern sky, each seemingly engaged in the ordering of a uniquely designed abstraction. It was the dreamscape of a mind out of focus fascinated by the ever-changing scene. The colors, a changing kaleidoscope, ranged from off-white to gray bleeding into black and to break the monotony a diversionary spot of pink gladdened the darkening sky. The river, stretched in a north-southerly direction, flowed along at its own tempo unconcerned with the drama overhead. The sun peaked through a momentary break in the cover, emitting rays in a crown of light to shimmer in silvery streaks on the moving waters. Suddenly cumulonimbus made an appearance to forecast the approaching storm.

"Was it Gen something? Oh yes, it has to be either 'ova' or 'eva.'" Marty heard Sonia say. "Where, oh where, did that same sky appear? Which was it: Geneva or Genova? Which? No, it couldn't be 'eva.' No, there the room had an ugly small window and buildings blocked the view of the lake. No, that Italian 'ova'—or is it English 'oa'—it makes no sense either way, for the hotel was too far from the sea. No, it has to be a wider scene? Out in the open. Think. Think. How about Morocco? I looked out from a parapet. Yes, that's it. The sun played around graying tufts of cotton-wool clouds. Streaks of light were poised over a patch of dark open water. God was it beautiful. Maybe it is really Morocco I'm thinking of. The rays remained out of reach as they dove into the ocean just as they have here. In Morocco it had been a magical moment, not threatening at all. Here it threatens. Why? But it does, it indeed feels threatening. I prefer Morocco." Sonia smiled.

Marty stood still, not wishing to intrude. He relaxed to wait.

"Look at that cloud," Sonia shouted, her eyes suddenly suffused with happiness. She stood up to brace herself against the window, her arms upraised, in an effort to touch the cloud. "It looks like Alex. It is Alex. How beautiful, almost like a perfect Roman facsimile of an Athenian. What is he doing up there?"

Sonia unexpectedly focused on Marty's reflection in the window glass. She was startled.

He was torn. He guessed she had been expecting an answer to her question—from whom? He was afraid to attempt a response.

"Who are you?" she said as she turned, her blue eyes fixed on him.

"It's me, Marty," he said as he tried to put on an unthreatening, friendly, cheerful face. "I'm your friend, Marty. I come every day. I'm your old, swarthy, friendly bookseller who can reach the highest shelf whenever you want a book. Remember?"

Marty held back. He started to scold himself. Why did you use the word that describes her problem? Shame. Everyone has individual quirks. Some of those affected, you've heard, become paranoid, some become uncontrollable, some refuse to wash or to eat or bits of all of these, but, for the time being Sonia still seems to have periods of lucidity, little windows that open up in the darkness of her mind. Yes, they are shrinking, but, at times, her memory is as clear as his. Sometime it vanishes into an abyss, wherever whatever opts to drag her along. At the moment she seems to be illusionary. In this room we never question memory. Naughty word, remember, don't use it! Alex up in the sky? Marty wished he could laugh. It is funny in a most unfunny sort of way, isn't it? He was pleased he had kept his promise to Alex to keep the nature of his illness hidden from Sonia in spite of the way she used to needle to try to elicit information about the personality changes she noticed, the loss of weight, the changed travel pattern and on and on until she stopped. But Alex as a cloud in the heavens when he was still very much a presence on earth was more than he could endure. To explain an image composed of droplets of water suspended in midair required an act of imagination. It would come, Marty was confident, inspiration would come, as it always seemed to come, on demand and unannounced.

"Leave me alone," Sonia said. It was almost a shout. "Who are you? A doctor—in blue jeans, yet. I've had the pleasure of one already, whenever it was today or yesterday on his daily round, asking impertinent questions. Go away." Her face turned into an ugly grimace.

"I will not stay if you don't want me to," Marty said, "But let me rest for a moment, will you? I've been standing all day. It wants to rain outside, and I've come a long way." He could almost see the adrenaline flowing through Sonia's system as she stiffened in a posture of defense against the intruder. He approached, moving as stealthily as he could until he stood by the chair facing her on the other side of the little round table and slowly lowered himself. He sensed she had relaxed and was pleased. He watched Sonia squint. He wondered if she was trying to enlarge the picture before her to examine it carefully. Her eyes slowly opened, reflecting a mind trying hard to place this stranger in friend's clothing who looked familiar. Without warning her face brightened.

"Of course, it's you, Marty. Yes, I know you. I know you well. So very well. So very long. Do sit next to me. Yes, there is fine," she said turning away from him to look out the window. She pointed to a big oval cloud, a mélange of pale white segueing into a series of grays melding into black as it rose up in the sky. "See that," she said. "It's Alex. What's he doing?"

"I don't think he's there," Marty said. She expected a response, and he wavered, uncertain what would satisfy her. He blurted, "He must have left already. He's just come home. He must have left a shadow behind. His way of sending you greetings, I guess, but transmission must have been delayed." He swallowed. He dared not tell her Alex was just out of hospital. "He's very imaginative in finding ways to communicate free of charge. Very clever of him."

"Where was he?" Sonia asked. She stopped as if trying to concentrate. As if counting her words, she said, "Do you—mean—Paris—again?"

"Yes." Marty decided that it was easier to agree than to contradict, although he wasn't pleased with the direction she was taking him. He was on guard but against what he wondered.

"I'd like to go to Paris one more time."

"When Alex comes, we'll talk. He promised to join me a little later." Marty scolded himself. You devil, you're putting off a response in the hope that this window of awareness will close, and she will forget all about Paris, hopefully before Alex comes who doesn't know he's supposed to have been there. Keep fingers crossed, he admonished himself. I hope it works.

"Is he coming? Do you think he'll tell me what he's been doing up there?"

"He wants to, of course, to say hello to you. He's a little tired; maybe jet lagged."

"Do you think he'll agree to going back with me, to Paris, one more time?"

"Let's talk when he gets here."

Sonia looked out the window. She seemed to be counting clouds. Her concentration was complete; she was oblivious of her surroundings. Marty did not budge. He wondered of what her world consisted.

"Just one more time to see Paris," Sonia piped up. "That's what I would like. I want to exit the *Métro*, the one by the, you know, the one leading to our street, with Alex holding my hand. I see us crossing the big avenue, going up the street, our street, into the courtyard—that's what it was, wasn't it, a courtyard? We greet the concierge, walk towards the back, veer to the left and up our stairs, open the door into the cold flat and walk straight back to the kitchen to put away the milk into the whatnot under the window. Wouldn't that be great?"

Sonia paused, lost in thought.

"Oh what, what, what, that what?" She stopped, searching for the elusive word. "What did we call the penicillin warder, the food protector, the outdoor pantry?" She giggled. "Of course, we called it a *mangyguard*, didn't we, in our version of *Franglais*. Did I invent that funny locution? I think I did. We didn't have a sophisticated electric box to keep food fresh, did we? One of those things we all have now. We used to have to shop all the time."

Sonia disappeared to collect thoughts that had strayed somehow. "What do you think it looks like today? Remember the Seine. Remember when we walked along the quay something or other, parallel to the museum. I think it was a museum—we were walking towards a great big gothic building. I can't think of the name of anything, but I can see it. Is this right? Can you see it? Did we cross a bridge to get over? We must have, didn't we? But I can still smell the dampness of our coats, of the river, of the sidewalk. We were meandering towards home, that apartment we called home. It had stopped drizzling. I wanted to photograph the sunset. It was so mind-bogglingly gorgeous. The clouds were cavorting something but not quite like now. I tried to find a place to set the camera down. You and Alex went off to a corner. You were so hungry all of a sudden. Why? What the hurry was all about you wouldn't say. You ignored me. You wouldn't help me find a place to set the camera. I hadn't taken the tripod, and I needed to time the exposure. You kept on walking. You hadn't even noticed I stopped. We got into a silly argument. We ended up in a café on the other side, eating baguette sandwiches. This was dinner in Paris before dinnertime. Can you believe? All I got for my trouble was a big blob on the negative. I got so mad at you both when we reached that café, consoling myself with a beer for dessert, that I walked off in a huff and went home. I'd like to go back and take it again."

"Good idea. Will you let me come with you and Alex?"

To Marty, Sonia was making sense. He wondered for how long. He wondered if it was the surge of unexpectedly remembered anger that cleared her mind. Or was it the sudden recollection of an incident long forgotten that was responsible. He wanted desperately to take advantage of the moment to unburden himself to tell her what he and Alex had been contemplating. Was it so wrong they wanted to go dancing where a man could dance with a man free to show his love? He would have liked after all these years to tell her it was not a place for girls, not nice girls, to clear the unfortunate misunderstanding, the ill will it created, that seemed to rankle still. And he hadn't even thought of it himself in such a long time. No, he couldn't. How could anyone know what thoughts were caroming through her mind—when—and if? And to think that so many years later, only now did he learn that the photograph he helped her take, which she looked forward to more than any other, had not come out. The one of the three of them, taken by the stranger on the bridge, which he had enlarged and cherished, was what he and Alex cared for. But to think she was still peeved at them. How wrong they had been, but, to his sorrow, he could not regret it. It remained one of his fondest memories of Paris, dancing with Alex in a sleazy joint.

Marty knew Sonia would never return to Paris. They had coaxed her into moving into the home when they determined on the advice of doctors she could no longer live by herself.

Absent any close family, they had no choice after the unexpected call from the fire department when she left the bacon smoldering on a burner while she went for the eggs she had forgotten to buy the evening before—wearing a raincoat crookedly buttoned over pajamas. There was no point in giving her any hope, even obliquely, she would ever see that city again.

The clouds triggered Sonia to try to recapture a similar sunset somewhere years ago. Marty thought he sort of did it too; maybe we all do it sometimes. But what of a place we once loved many, many years ago? Can we recapture it? Most likely it is not the same; it may not even be recognizable. We can describe it; we can repopulate it in our mind's eye; we can write about it; but we can never physically inhabit it again. If we did, it would by necessity be a different experience in a city by a quirk of existence using the same name.

Although Sonia had been to the *Marais* more than once since it had been refashioned—what's the term?—

gentrified?—in the shadow of the *Pompidou Center*, that industrial superstructure in the guise of a museum of modern art, what she wanted to visit is the neighborhood as it used to be when she was young. It was an image of a working-class quarter, of a vanished past. Marty thought back and counted. A mere half century had elapsed since then. How could he say anything? He didn't even know if she would be rational enough to put herself together to go anywhere. He wished he could do it for her, but he didn't think it was feasible.

"Marty, where were you? Day dreaming? Rehearsing a soliloquy? Tell me about it." Sonia looked enquiringly at Marty.

"Good of you to wake me up. You made me think of Paris—that's where I was. All your fault." Marty's tearing eyes revealed his emotions as a crooked smile said it all, if only Sonia could still read him as she used to.

"Do I really want to go back to Paris? Is that what you're thinking?" Sonia said. "Let's wait for Alex. What I'm thinking of is ineffable memory. What does ineffable mean? I guess it means it can't be described. If I can't express it, do I remember it? Does it mean that it's in my head but I can't put it into words? If I can't verbalize it, I can't retrieve it. The conundrum about the tree falling in the forest; if there is nobody to see it, has it fallen. I don't know." Sonia giggled as if revealing a secret. "I guess that's what's happening to me, sometimes, frequently maybe, more often all the time. I can't remember. Yes, I even don't remember I can't remember when I remember?"

Marty was stunned. Nobody, the doctors, Alex, their friends, certainly he, had ever guessed that Sonia was aware of the nature of her illness. Here, he heard it described in so many words. He wanted to say something, whatever it be, to offer comfort, understanding, support, but he couldn't think of anything that wouldn't turn into meaningless words.

Sonia concentrated on the clouds out the window now releasing torrents of rain; she could have been requesting advice from the elements. After an interminable moment she continued. "I may have the equivalent of the crumbling madeleine dipped in tea to prod my memory—maybe. When there is any memory to prod, that is, and I am conscious of the prod. Incidentally, remember when we stopped, you and I, at the pastry shop up the street to try the madeleine with tea? The lady was incredulous we would come just for that. She won. We ended up after soggy cake with delicious tarts. The madeleine meant nothing to us, except Proust and his little book. Ha! Not so little. But now it is the coffee shop and the tarts that mean something to us. Remember the raspberry tart? But, of course, this is not real Proustian memory; it's not involuntary memory; it's voluntary recollection. The only similarity to his is that my trigger is increasingly preceded by oblivion. Do I mean increasing oblivion or increasingly preceded? And trigger to what? Maybe it is a difference without a distinction. I don't know. I doubt he and I have the same mental condition in mind—similarities notwithstanding. A different name, but I can't think of it." Sonia harrumphed.

"Yes, I do remember the pastry shop," answered Marty. Although he could have grasped the moment to attempt to learn how her mind worked, he held back. He didn't want to intrude. Was it to penetrate into her soul that he wanted? He wasn't sure. Perhaps it was merely to get a glint of the mechanics of how her mind had deteriorated. Weird were the ways of dementia. He said, "It was on the way to the Opera that we found it, that shop, on a little street, but I'm no longer sure which corner or which street."

"I'm not sure either. But I can see her. She was heavyset, short dark hair, sort of frizzy, very polite. I loved her greeting, '*Bonjourmessieursdames.*' All one blurred word. She thought we were a bit odd. But you know, sometimes that river outside my window does just as well to remind me of the Seine—sort of. My Paris is always with me. But what will I find if I go back? That's what frightens me. I don't want to see another Paris. I want my own. Maybe it's not worthwhile going back. Just sit here and remember and dream of the beautiful sunset I never captured on film. Those clouds decorating the sky in all those reds and purples against the artsy bridge—scuse, please, the *Pont des Arts*—is that the right bridge?—were magnificent."

Sonia looked directly at Marty, but he didn't think she saw him. Her eyes suddenly looked blank. Perhaps she had abandoned him for what she was retrieving from her recollection of the City of Light.

Marty realized he had again become invisible. His thoughts wandered off taking inventory of his surroundings to ascertain if they were familiar and still there. He took in the tidy institutional bed next to the night table with the box of tissues, no longer the customary book she was in the habit of taking to bed with her before falling asleep. The door to the bathroom always slightly ajar offended him for the easy access it invited in case of uncontrollable need. The mirror over the chest of drawers against the wall next to the bathroom reflected a fresh array of red roses gracing a courtesy-of-florist cheap glass vase. A fresh bouquet of flowers arrived every fifth day on standing orders from Alex to the neighborhood florist, the one Sonia used to patronize. The room was antiseptic, impersonal, except for the touch of color emanating from the flowers.

"Shall I call for tea?" Sonia's voice erupted as if she had awakened from a long sleep.

"Is it teatime?" countered Marty.

"I don't know if it is. What I really would like is a martini. If it's not teatime, it has to be, I know, happy hour. That's it. Let's call for a martini."

"You want a martini? My name, full name, legal name, is Martin, as you know. If we add an 'I' to it, it becomes 'martini.' Won't I do?"

"You're trying to be punny. I mean punny, not funny at all. You are not succeeding. Besides which you stole the pun. It was mine. I used to call you that, sometimes. What I want now, a martini, the drink, the one Alex likes to drink."

Marty felt compelled to interject a different idea, although he wasn't sure what she did or did not know about Alex. Aside from the fact that it used to be true, he wanted to get her off the subject of martinis.

"You know he doesn't drink anymore, martinis or anything else."

"So what! That's his problem if he doesn't want to indulge. He always made the most wonderful martinis. Just the right amount of vermouth, that's the secret."

Marty was concerned that a mouthful of alcohol injected into her bloodstream could turn her in an instant into an uncontrollable drunk. The effect on an unstable mind was, as he had discovered, unnerving. That it was not on the nursing-home menu is something he knew, and she in her rational moments realized. The fact was alcoholic drinks were no longer part of her diet.

"Well," Sonia said.

"Well, what?" Amanda, her nurse, said. She had appeared in their midst just in time on rubber-soled shoes, without warning, as if dropped from the heavens.

"Hi, Nurse Amanda," Marty said. "I'm delighted to see you looking ravishing as usual."

"Hello, Marty. Compliments and the proverbial token will get you into the subway. But thanks anyway. Always good to see you. It's dinner time. Why didn't you tell me you were coming? I haven't ordered dinner for you. The table is set, not including you. But we can pull up a chair if you would like to accompany us."

"Thanks, not tonight. Alex should be here soon. He and I are going to dinner afterwards."

"You need the bathroom?" Amanda asked Sonia.

"No," Sonia said.

"What do you need?" Amanda said.

"Leave me alone. I want to go home," Sonia said.

"But you are home," Marty said. He stood up, walked around the little table to where Sonia was sitting and put his arm around her. She raised herself to stand next to him and said, "This is not home. Where is he who looks after us children?"

Amanda spoke to her directly, holding her hand while massaging it. She said, "Here is Marty. Here am I. We're family. We look after each other. This is home."

"I want my coat. I want to go home. Home to mother," Sonia said, as if those around her were hard of hearing, uncomprehending of her stated demands.

Marty guided her closer towards the window. "Look at your friends, the clouds. See what they are doing. It's raining hard outside. You want to wait until it clears before going out. When it clears and the stars twinkle, we will decide. Agree?"

Sonia returned to the armchair in front of the window she had left a minute ago. Marty remained standing. She quieted down as she began once again to concentrate on the clouds and the storm outside. Suddenly she jumped up, having become aware of the reflection of Alex in the window. He was standing behind her. She veered around and flung herself into his arms.

"Whoa there, lady. You almost threw me down."

Marty rushed up to them. Sonia was hanging unto Alex. Marty took her by the waist and gently supported her. He held her until her arms relaxed and she let go of Alex's neck so he could bring her down. She stood glued to Alex, glowing with joy.

Marty was amazed by the transformation before him as he was every time he was witness to it. He remembered Sonia's young eyes, enormous and blue they were then, when she emerged to join Alex to go to the opera that afternoon long ago in Paris. The eyes, although sadly diminished by the inevitable droop of her aging eyelids, were still blue, radiating even more, if it were possible, that admixture of happiness to be alive and desire the instant she sensed the presence of Alex. The smile with which she approached the young Alex, the Alex with the lock of blond hair falling on his forehead, was the same that illuminated her face now. Alex was tall, still tall, but not as tall as he had been. He was thin, thinner because of the degeneration due to his disease and the action of the cocktail of drugs intended to counteract it. Marty assumed he saw the hair as blond still although now much lighter because of the admixture of gray. The vestige of the handsome visage concentrated in his piercing blue-gray eyes was all that remained of what had been. Marty was convinced that to Sonia the changes were insignificant.

"Alex, is it really you?" Sonia cried out. "I can't believe you are here. Come with me. Look up at the sky. See that cloud? You were there a minute ago. Why? What were you doing?" She pulled him towards the window and wouldn't let go.

Marty observed a scenario he had seen many times with recently acquired complacency. Sonia, the bolt of lightning having struck, became energized the moment Alex appeared. She radiated the delight of a young woman in love. She instantly relaxed as if the cares of the world had been transferred from her shoulders unto Alex. She was happy, illness an invisible blip on the horizon. This time, he prayed the bloom would not fade as the moment played out.

"Show me," Alex gently coaxed. "Or better still, tell me what you saw. There is nothing there now. All I see is the storm that got me wet."

"It's gone," Sonia said. "I guess it went. But earlier there was a gorgeous you up in the sky. You were still there, sort of, when Marty arrived. Can you tell me how you got there? You were in Paris. Did you reach up to the"—she stumbled—"the clcclclouds to say hello to me?

Marty told me you just came back, so I knew you had to have been in Paris. How was it, my Paris?"

"Yes, Alex, sorry I blurted your secret before you could tell Sonia yourself," Marty said. He gazed directly at Alex trusting his eyes would transmit the emergency message he did not have time to convey. "It spurted out of me when I tried to explain why you couldn't use your cell phone. I'm sorry. Am I forgiven?"

"You are a funny man, my dear Marty. Of course, you are forgiven. Now what shall I say about Paris?" Alex paused and turned to the clouds as if trying to read whatever message he could decipher, maybe even discover which cloud resembled him. He finally said. "Your Paris is still the Paris you love. What more can I tell you?"

"Don't confuse me. You were up in the sky before and now you are here. Marty also saw you. He can vouch for me. Why were you in Paris?"

"It was the usual. Now I'm home. I'm talking to you. You are lovely."

"Thanks for the compliment. But I want to talk Paris with you. Yes, Paris. I want to go back and see it one more time. Just one more time. Will you go with me?" She turned to Marty, "You can leave your bookstore alone for a week, can't you, and come with us. We have to go together, we three. For me."

Sonia stopped talking and admired Alex. Nothing clever was said; conversation subsided, peace reigned among them. Marty could not think of what to do to derail the subject of Paris, but it occurred to him that he was tired. Being with Sonia for more than an hour had become exhausting—a new development. He realized part of it could be age, part of it could be the progression of her illness making communication difficult. Yes, he would continue to come visit, as would Alex. He noted Sonia looking from him to Alex and back again. The three of them stood by the window presumably engrossed by the storm. Marty put his mouth to Alex's ear to whisper he was ready to leave any time he was.

"Hey you! Congratulations! You two are plotting, and you think I don't know what's going on. You did it before. You are going to abandon me. I see myself trying to take a photograph. Why didn't you help me? What am I recalling? What am I seeing so vividly? Why?" Tears sprang to Sonia's eyes. She crumpled unto her chair. "Where am I?" she cried.

"You are in New York, at home," Alex said. "Why do you cry? No need to cry." He put his arm around her, lifted her, clasped her body to his. He stroked her hair.

"I'll get Amanda," Marty said, having noticed she had disappeared when Alex arrived. He rushed to the nurses' station.

When Marty returned with Amanda, she came with capsules in a little paper cup and a glass of water. "Look what we have here? Our favorite elixir to make us feel better. Dear, oh dear, why do we cry?" Amanda said. She gently moved Alex's arm away from Sonia and put her own around her shoulder. She turned her away from Alex and emptied the capsules in the cup into Sonia's left hand, placed the glass in her right hand, and motioned to Marty and Alex to go.

"Dear Sonia," Marty said. "I'll be back tomorrow."

Sonia brought herself down slowly into the chair. Her attention diverted, she ignored her guests to concentrate on the glass of water and the drugs before her. She had returned to her own mysterious world.

Marty waved and led Alex out the door. "Let's go have some dinner," he said.

They walked down the corridor holding hands.

"Are you alright?" Marty asked. "You seem to forget you came out of hospital day before yesterday the way you carry on. Maybe you shouldn't have come."

"I sat in the lobby for quite a while. I was out of breath and didn't want to face Sonia. She might guess something is wrong."

"That's why you look so fresh. I notice your shoes are quite wet."

"Anyway, Sonia was glad to see me. You told her I'd been in Paris? Clever. I love the humor of being questioned on a trip I never dreamed of taking." Alex's face brightened. "You will do anything to protect Sonia. I love you for that. Now, what was this about me in the sky?"

"You tell me, if you will, how a portrait can be created by clouds? Or did she mean you were literally in the clouds? I can't remember which she was talking about when. I think both. How I got around it I'm not sure. When I suggested you had wanted to say hello, her mind seemed to have cleared somewhat, ergo you'd been in Paris. What to say? She then almost rationally reminisced about our life in and around the apartment, and how much she'd like to see Paris once more with both of us. This led her to reflection on memory, allusion to Proust and such. But she almost had it right when she started speaking about the various kinds of memory and threw in ineffable memory. She described her disease in such detail without naming it frightened me. And yet, she confuses me. Her last outburst just before we left, I swear, seemed to me to be a Proustian epiphany. Was it? Is it in some way a form of dementia or connected to it? I can't help but wonder. We'll find out, I guess, when the time comes, if the doctors do an autopsy. I mean what kind of dementia she has. In life, in practice, dementias behave more or less the same. I doubt the name makes a difference. But Proustian involuntary memory may be another matter—or is it? We may get another clue if and when she has another similar recall."

Marty watched Alex carefully. Alex could become emotionally erratic because he was physically weak. He worried. He worried about Alex. He worried about Sonia. He was despondent and yet no longer felt free to confide in Alex. He certainly couldn't talk to Sonia. He muttered, "A great end to our trio and our occasional duets, one with AIDS, one with ineffable memory, and me. How I escaped is beyond me."

Marty barely heard Alex say under his breath, "I'm afraid you'll have to learn to play solo." Alex stopped. Marty felt Alex grasp his hand as if with a vise, as if afraid to be abandoned. He shivered. Alex whispered releasing a tangle of words until there were no more. "Maybe one day she'll blurt out the truth. There is *Puno*, of course. I hope not. One never knows."

They exited unto the street, walked to the corner and stopped to wait for the light to change. Alex did not let go of Marty's hand. They crossed over in the direction of Second Avenue. Alex continued, "I assume you remember the letter she told me she wrote you from *Iquitos*. She was supposed to describe how we ended up sharing a double bed because of a scarcity of rooms due to an uprising we could not have anticipated. We did more than clasp hands across a non-existent divide. She meant to explain. She told me she would refer to Proust—not to share him with you but to mislead you—to the scene where Swann preparing to possess Odette imagines himself a voyager ready to depart never to return. Did she succeed? I feel like adding virginal to describe Odette, but she was certainly not a virgin although I guess maybe he would have liked her to be and, of course, what is implied is that he sees her as a virgin. I'm not sure I'm making sense. Did I get the Proust right? Maybe not. But I trust you to understand. Yes, we betrayed you. We never imagined we'd fall prey that night to full hotels, curfews, armies. I blame what happened on the Peruvian elixir. I never had that wine again. I never referred to that trip." Alex chuckled.

They ambled on, glad the rain had stopped. Marty was silent as they continued to walk hand in hand. As they approached the avenue, Alex continued, "The truth is she didn't want to lose you. That's why the letter. I'm glad neither of us did. We were a happy trio. I couldn't live without you. I doubt Sonia could have existed without you. Why she remained obsessed with me, I'll never know, but I guess I returned the favor. Perhaps you have always known the truth, would not indicate you knew, to us, maybe not even to yourself. That's why I have always loved you, but then I could never live without you, no matter what else I let myself do."

They exited onto the avenue in the direction of the restaurant. Marty was silent. Alex let go of Marty's hand. Marty glanced at Alex. *No need to worry*, he seemed to say. Marty looked up at the clearing sky. Wispy clouds. A misty aura. Lamplight reflected on a wet sidewalk. A mirage. Paris, the *Café des deux Magots*, across the street from the church of *Saint-Germaine des Près*. An image. Three figures, one woman, two men, walking arm in arm. Marty smiled. He relaxed. He clutched Alex's hand.

ABOUT ATMOSPHERE PRESS

Atmosphere Press is an independent, full-service publisher for excellent books in all genres and for all audiences. Learn more about what we do at atmospherepress.com.

We encourage you to check out some of Atmosphere's latest releases, which are available at Amazon.com and via order from your local bookstore:

The Tattered Black Book, a novel by Lexy Duck
The Red Castle, a novel by Noah Verhoeff
American Genes, a novel by Kirby Nielsen
Newer Testaments, a novel by Philip Brunetti
All Things in Time, a novel by Sue Buyer
Hobson's Mischief, a novel by Caitlin Decatur
The Black-Marketer's Daughter, a novel by Suman Mallick
The Farthing Quest, a novel by Casey Bruce
This Side of Babylon, a novel by James Stoia
Within the Gray, a novel by Jenna Ashlyn
For a Better Life, a novel by Julia Reid Galosy
Where No Man Pursueth, a novel by Micheal E. Jimerson
Here's Waldo, a novel by Nick Olson
Tales of Little Egypt, a historical novel by James Gilbert
The Hidden Life, a novel by Robert Castle
Big Beasts, a novel by Patrick Scott
Alvarado, a novel by John W. Horton III
Nothing to Get Nostalgic About, a novel by Eddie Brophy

ABOUT THE AUTHOR

Miriam Malach is a writer living in New York City.

CPSIA information can be obtained
at www.ICGtesting.com
Printed in the USA
LVHW091711040521
686471LV00009B/656